Critical Guides to French Texts

Critical Guides to French Texts

EDITED BY ROGER LITTLE, WOLFGANG VAN EMDEN, DAVID WILLIAMS

BEAUMARCHAIS

Le Mariage de Figaro

Second Edition

Robert Niklaus

Emeritus Professor of French,
University of Exeter

Grant & Cutler Ltd
1995

© Grant & Cutler Ltd 1995

ISBN 0 7293 0378 0

First edition 1983

Second edition 1995

I.S.B.N. 84-499-6346-X

DEPÓSITO LEGAL: V. 529 - 1995

Printed in Spain by
Artes Gráficas Soler, S.A., Valencia
for
GRANT & CUTLER LTD
55–57 GREAT MARLBOROUGH STREET, LONDON W1V 2AY

Contents

Contents

Foreword

The italicised arabic numerals in brackets refer to works fully described in the bibliography.

References to the text of the play are to the Bordas edition (*10*), first published in 1964 and readily available. The lines of this text have been numbered from 1 to 3214, so as to facilitate the identification of any quotation. This edition provides a detailed chronology of events in the life of Beaumarchais. For a chronology that runs in parallel columns facts in the life of Beaumarchais, significant historical events, literary landmarks and intellectual, religious and artistic milestones, reference may be made to the Hachette edition (*12*) published in 1986. No chronology, however, can be wholly satisfactory in the case of a life as complex as that of Beaumarchais, for unavoidable contraction can often prove misleading to anyone unfamiliar with the involved pattern of Beaumarchais's activities. The best biography to date is that by P. Richard (*32*), but since its publication new information has come to light and in particular that presented by J. Donvez (*47*). The best edition of *Le Mariage de Figaro* is undoubtedly that by J.-P. de Beaumarchais (*13*), a descendant of the playwright, who has been in a position to consult the family archives. It has the advantage of comprising *Le Sacristain*, a recently discovered *intermède* or sketch which has close links with *Le Barbier de Séville*, *Le Barbier* itself, *Le Mariage de Figaro* and *La Mère coupable*. In his introduction J.-P. de Beaumarchais has stressed the connection between the three substantial plays that form what one may call the *Figaro trilogy*.

1. Introduction

When on 27 April 1784 the curtain rose for the first time on the stage of the Comédie Française on a performance of *Le Mariage de Figaro*, Beaumarchais had already made his mark as a playwright with *Eugénie ou la Vertu malheureuse* (1767), *Les Deux Amis ou le Négociant de Lyon* (1770), both *drames bourgeois* in the prevailing contemporary mould, and *Le Barbier de Séville* (1775) which had won wide acclaim. *Le Mariage de Figaro* was an outstanding triumph with a first run of 68 performances and 100 performances by 1787, an unprecedented achievement in the eighteenth century. Receipts amounted to 346,197 *livres* of which 293,755 were awarded to the actors whilst the author's own share amounted to 41,499 *livres*. The play was quickly performed in the provinces and translated into English, German, Russian, Polish and other languages. At the Comédie Française revivals soon followed and the play was to become one of the most popular at France's national theatre. By 31 December 1981 no fewer than *1249* performances were recorded there, the most recent in 1977 and again in 1978 with J. Rosser as producer. In 1956-57 Jean Vilar gave a memorable production at the Théâtre National Populaire, and in 1964 Jean-Louis Barrault had the work included in the repertoire of the Théâtre de France. In 1980 Françoise Petit produced the play for the Théâtre de Paris. *Le Mariage de Figaro* has been turned into a film by Jean Meyer and the Company of the Comédie Française, and has been shown in at least two distinctive productions on the French television network. In England Thomas Holcroft managed to secure an imperfect copy of the play which he turned into *Follies of a day*, a play in three acts performed with some success in December 1784 and frequently since. Is it necessary to add that in 1786 Mozart composed his opera *Le Nozze di Figaro* on a libretto by Lorenzo Da Ponte which follows very closely the text of Beaumarchais's play (see bibliography, *42*), and which has been considered by some as Mozart's finest work? The phenomenal success of *La Folle Journée ou Le Mariage de Figaro*, to give the full title as it appears on the title page of the first published edition of the play authorised by Beaumarchais (1785), cannot be called in question. People queued to see the play from 11 a.m. till 4 p.m. when the box office opened on the first night; there was a stampede, attendants were brushed aside and three people are said to have died of suffocation. The applause was so great that the performance took 5 hours instead of 3½. To account for this triumph it is necessary to subject the various aspects of the play to careful scrutiny. By so doing it is hoped to bring out its true nature and assess its merit. To date there are as many interpretations of the play as there are critics. This testimony to its vitality often baffles the reader. The multiplicity of points of view that can legitimately be entertained reflects of course the personal preferences and sometimes the limitations of the critics. There are those who would judge the play in the light of accepted canons going back in time to Aristotle and the Greeks, or more specifically French classical drama. For them it is comparatively easy to record how far *Le Mariage* falls short of a theoretical perfection. Others like Francine Levy (*26*) insist on seeing in its political utterances its chief claim to significance. Nearly all find in the personality of Beaumarchais the key to and the chief source of its success, whilst one or two are content to present an interpretation that excludes all extraneous matters and to stick closely to the written text (Pugh, *21*). These several approaches all have validity and are by no means exclusive, although they may have frequently led to misleading conclusions. It is only recently that we have come to think of the play essentially as theatre and apply to its study the criteria of the theatre. For us the play as performed will be our main concern[1] and criticism based solely on a reading of the play will be recognised as valid only when the critic has shown enough imagination to visualize the scenes as enacted. Speculation must surely be put to the test of practical experience and we may well find that peculiarities or obscurities of language need to be examined in the light of their

[1] Meyer (*19*) and Scherer (*9*) are particularly helpful in this respect.

effectiveness on the stage, as in the case of Molière's *galimatias*. For on the stage the drift of an actor's speech may be conveyed very clearly in a given situation by idiomatic or familiar expressions, even neologisms and loosely constructed sentences, when it is accompanied by facial expression and gesture, whilst it will elude the myopic reader seeking precise definition and on the look-out for possible confusion.

Certainly from the original cast in 1784 which Beaumarchais praised unstintingly to that of recent years a succession of fine actors has brought life to the comedy in spite of or perhaps because of its eighteenth-century setting. Actors of high calibre are drawn to the play as a challenge to their ability and a means of consecrating their reputation. *Le Mariage de Figaro* attracts wide audiences, a wider spectrum of theatregoers than either Marivaux's or Musset's best plays and Beaumarchais may be ranked immediately after Molière among the great French writers of comedy. Beaumarchais's reputation, however, rests on only two plays, *Le Barbier de Séville* and *Le Mariage de Figaro*, the latter being generally considered to be the better.

2. Genesis of the work

A. Historical and Biographical

It took a struggle lasting many years to secure the right to have the play performed. Already in 1775 and prompted by his patron and friend the Prince de Conti who urged him to stage a sequel to *Le Barbier de Séville*, Beaumarchais decided to portray the same characters in a new situation on the lines of his somewhat fanciful proposal in his *Lettre modérée* which was a spirited defence of *Le Barbier de Séville*. He must have begun work on *Le Mariage* soon after the death of the Prince in 1776 and certainly before 1778 when he may well have determined its essential features. On 29 September 1781 the play was submitted to the actors of the Comédie Française who received it with enthusiasm. The censor Coqueley de Chaussepierre had no qualms in passing it as suitable for public performance and a copy was forwarded to the Court where Marie Antoinette read it with enjoyment and requested Madame Campan to read it to Louis XVI. The latter judged the play to be in bad taste, disliking its Italian *concetti* and taking violent exception to the famous monologue in Act V, scene 3 (2679-779). He is reported to have exclaimed: 'C'est détestable. Cela ne sera jamais joué; il faudrait détruire la Bastille pour que la représentation de cette pièce ne fût pas une inconséquence dangereuse.' It is important, however, to point out that the King was greatly offended by the text of the first draft of the monologue in which the action takes place in France and in which the Bastille is specifically mentioned. In other passages, later suppressed, Beaumarchais overtly attacked the clergy and the censorship.[2]

Beaumarchais's immediate response was to situate the play explicitly at Aguas-Frescas, in Spain, as he had done in the case

[2] See the additional passages found in Beaumarchais's papers which E. Lintilhac (*30*) published for the first time in vol. IV of his *Histoire générale du théâtre en France*, pp.434 *et seq.*

of *Le Barbier de Séville*, and to cut out a few offending passages and effect minor alterations. The ban on the performance of the play gained the author much publicity which he exploited to the full. He began to read his manuscript in the salons, in particular to the Archduke of Russia, the future Tsar Paul II, and the Archduchess, the Princesse de Lamballe, the Maréchal de Richelieu and other prominent people. A second censor, Suard, was appointed who gave an adverse ruling, as could have been expected. Beaumarchais, who was at the time in London on a delicate mission, then heard that his play was to be performed at the Théâtre des Menus-Plaisirs by the actors of the Comédie Française in the presence of the Comte d'Artois, brother of the King. But once again Louis XVI forbade the performance for fear of appearing to vacillate and establishing a dangerous precedent.

The curiosity of the public was now thoroughly aroused and the King was soon forced to yield to public clamour first by allowing the play to be put on in the private theatre of Gennevilliers which belonged to the Comte de Vandreuil, for the special benefit of the Comte d'Artois, then by yielding to Beaumarchais's request that a third censor, Gaillard, should be appointed so as to place Suard in a minority. The final report left Louis XVI little option but to signify his approval. Thus *La Folle Journée ou Le Mariage de Figaro* came to be performed for the first time on 26 September 1783.[3] The Comte d'Artois and the Duchesse de Polignac freely expressed their enthusiasm for the play. Three new censors were now appointed: the first expressed reservations on moral grounds, the second was over-eulogistic, the third confined himself to approval without comment. And so it came to pass that at last, on 31 March 1784, Beaumarchais was in a position to write to the actor Fréville who had ensured the success of *Le Barbier de Séville*: 'J'ai, mon vieil ami, le *bon* du roi, le *bon* du ministre, le *bon* du lieutenant de police: il ne me manque plus que le vôtre pour voir un beau tapage à la rentrée' (quoted in *4*, 1957 ed., p.675). On 27 April 1784 the play was performed by the Comédiens du Roi in a new

---

[3] E.J. Arnould (*5*, p.xxii) states that the first performance was actually on 18 September 1783. He may have been referring to a 'dress rehearsal'.

auditorium where for the first time there were seats in the pit and reflector lamps to replace the candles of the old Salle des Tuileries. The resounding success not only vindicated Beaumarchais but became the occasion of an apotheosis. The prolonged banning of the play and all the advance publicity, the excellence of the acting and above all the unquestioned merit of the work played their part in ensuring the author's triumph. Women of quality went to see the play in *petites loges* where they would not be recognised so as to enjoy, according to Beaumarchais, 'les plaisirs du vice et honneurs de la vertu'.

Beaumarchais never accepted that his play was morally equivocal. The censor Suard, part owner of the *Journal de Paris* and a journalist on the staff of the *Gazette de France*, continued to attack the play anonymously. Beaumarchais invariably replied to any criticism on the principle that further publicity could do nothing but good; but he caused some irritation in the entourage of the King. Exception was taken in particular to a sentence in which Beaumarchais declared that if needs be he would have his play performed in the choir of Notre Dame and that he had had to overcome the opposition of lions and tigers to get his play staged. The King felt affronted and had him incarcerated at Saint-Lazare, a gaol chiefly used to punish cheeky adolescents who deserved to be caned. For a while people laughed, but soon realised that if arbitrary imprisonment on such trivial grounds became the rule they would themselves be vulnerable. Four days after his incarceration, on 8 March 1785, he was released and Louis XVI had 800,000 *livres* paid to him in belated compensation for the loss of a merchant fleet he had raised to help the American insurgents and as a reward for his action in their support, but also no doubt for the indignity he had suffered. Marie Antoinette arranged for a performance of *Le Barbier de Séville*, with music by Paesiello, which took place on 19 August 1785 and which Beaumarchais was invited to attend. The Queen herself played the part of Rosine.

On 18 August *Le Mariage* was given its 74th performance before Ministers of the King. Beaumarchais had now reached the peak of his career. His subsequent involvement in a quarrel with Mirabeau did not redound to his credit, the Congress of the

United States, whilst expressing thanks for his aid, only made vague promises of payment which were not kept, and his espousal of the case of Mme Kornmann who had been forsaken by her husband exposed him to the slanders of a lawyer called Bergasse and held him up to public ridicule. His unexpected excursion into philosophical opera, *Tarare* (performed on 8 June 1787) had only an ephemeral success and the advent of the French Revolution led him to being accused of trafficking in arms. His sumptuous home standing close to the Bastille did not endear him to the militants. He found himself once again incarcerated and was deprived of his property. He was saved from the guillotine only by the intercession of a woman admirer. He left for Holland, then went on to London. He was eventually rehabilitated and, after a short stay in Paris, went abroad on a mission on behalf of the Comité de Salut Public. He was then placed on a list of *émigrés* and had to flee to Hamburg. The Directoire authorised his return to Paris on 5 July 1796.

His *comédie larmoyante*, tearful or sentimental *drame*, *L'Autre Tartuffe, ou La Mère coupable*, the third and last of his plays dealing with Figaro, had been performed with indifferent success on 26 June 1792; now it was revived to public acclaim on 5 May 1797. In 1785, after a liaison lasting twelve years Beaumarchais married Mlle de Willermaulaz, a motherly Swiss lady of distinction, doubtless to legitimise his daughter Eugénie; but it must be remembered that Beaumarchais had had to fight long to reacquire his full rights as a citizen and until he had won his case he could not legally enter into a contract of marriage. Mlle de Willermaulaz coped well with Beaumarchais's frequent infidelities and behaved with great dignity. She gave him a home and a sense of security which brought him comfort in his last years. He died in Paris on 18 May 1799 of a stroke, and, as he himself had requested, was buried in his own garden.

There is growing interest today in *La Mère coupable*, a *drame* in five acts, as a sequel to *Le Mariage de Figaro* and for the light it can throw on Beaumarchais's own evaluation of his characters and their destiny, but also as an example of a genre now dead, yet of considerable historical interest in that it blurred the distinction between tragedy and comedy, reflected new social

tendencies and heralded both melodrama and romantic drama.[4]
La Mère coupable had a chequered career. Accepted for
performance by the Comédie Française it was shelved owing to a
disagreement over the author's rights. It was then handed to the
actors of the Théâtre du Marais. During Beaumarchais's
absence abroad his friends brought out an expurgated version of
the play with M. and Mme Almaviva and their son M. Léon now
no longer to be considered aristocrats. *La Mère coupable*
certainly marks a sad decline in Beaumarchais's genius and his
characters have lost their vitality and their appeal. He tried to
link *Tarare*, his other late work, with Figaro and wrote: 'Comme
Figaro, Tarare échappe à tous les pièges, arrache sa femme aux
mains d'Atar et est couronné par acclamation'. But the linkage
is far-fetched, for *Tarare* does not seem to have much in common with *Le Mariage*.

In 1784 Beaumarchais's future career as outlined above was
scarcely an object of speculation. The spectators were drawn to
Le Mariage not only because of the years of publicity that had
preceded the performance and the known brilliance of the
author, but also by a certain fascination with his personality and
what was known of his multifarious activities. In Court circles
he was known as the son of a clockmaker who had followed in
his father's footsteps and invented an escapement movement in
1753 which Lepaute had claimed as his own, but which the
Académie des Sciences finally attributed to Augustin Caron, to
give Beaumarchais his first name. The style of de Beaumarchais
was assumed in 1756 upon his marriage to a widow, Mme
Franquet, who had a property of that name. He was welcomed
at Versailles where he gave lessons on the harp to the daughters
of Louis XV.

In 1761 he became *secrétaire du roi* and was awarded a title
together with 85,000 *livres*. He acquired the office of
'Lieutenant général des chasses aux baillages et capitainerie de
La Varenne du Louvre', which must have provided him with
first-hand experience of legal procedure. He frequented finan-
ciers like Pâris-Duverney who initiated him into the complexity

---

[4] See p.24 for further information on *le drame* as a source of Beaumarchais's
play.

of the business world, and in 1770 made him a beneficiary under his will. He frequented another financier, Lenormant d'Etioles, the husband of Mme de Pompadour, and performed his own *parades* at his private theatre. His numerous activities, carried on simultaneously, could not have been widely known, but they are important in that they show Beaumarchais as a man of intrigue who would be at home in the complicated plots and counterplots of his plays. One example of relevance to the background of *Le Barbier* and *Le Mariage* will suffice to bring out this aspect of his life. In 1764 he went to Madrid ostensibly to avenge the honour of his sister Lisette who had been jilted by a Spanish journalist Clavijo, but at the same time to secure commercial openings for Pâris-Duverney in the newly acquired Spanish province of Louisiana. He even envisaged trafficking in slaves, showing that self-interest was of greater importance to him than the new ideology. He also contrived to establish his own mistress as the mistress of the Spanish monarch in a shady diplomatic move to further his standing with the King of France. His Spanish adventure provided him with more than the Spanish setting for *Le Barbier de Séville*, for it gave him the name, profession and character of Figaro himself.[5]

His involvement in intrigue, however, seems to have become known and his own philandering gave him a scandalous reputation which his marriage to a rich widow in April 1768 followed by her death on 21 November 1770 did nothing to diminish. It was his quarrel with his friend the Duc de Chaulnes over a woman for which he was incarcerated at For-l'Evêque (1773), and especially the *affaire La Blache* that brought him wide notoriety. Upon the death of Pâris-Duverney, on 17 July 1770, his heir, the Comte de La Blache, contested his uncle's will in respect of a legacy to Beaumarchais and challenged the authenticity of a signature, accusing Beaumarchais of forgery. In 1772 the Court pronounced in Beaumarchais's favour on the strength of a document signed by Pâris-Duverney on 1st April 1770, but La Blache decided to appeal. Judge Goëzman was appointed *rapporteur* on 1st April 1773 and Beaumarchais, having obtained permission to leave For-l'Evêque for the purpose (4-5

[5] See p.40.

April), visited the home of Mme Goëzman to whom he made a
present of a diamond-studded watch as well as 100 *louis*, fifteen
of which were to go to her secretary. On 6 April the Parlement
reversed the original verdict and ordered Beaumarchais to pay
56,300 *livres* and costs. His property was confiscated in payment. Mme Goëzman then returned the watch and 85 *louis*, retaining the fifteen *louis* of the secretary. Filled with indignation,
Beaumarchais wrote four virulent *Mémoires* which deal with the
misdemeanours of the Goëzman family and his own grievances.
These constitute a masterpiece of polemical writing and won
over the reading public to his cause. His contemporaries, well-
accustomed to the practice of bribing judges, noted chiefly the
immorality of Mme Goëzman in retaining the fifteen *louis*, and
the witty argumentation of the author. Sixteen days after the
publication of the last *Mémoire*, Beaumarchais embarked on a
suit against Goëzman which was taken to court, and on 26
February 1774 Mme Goëzman was suitably reprimanded and
Beaumarchais deprived of his civic rights. Goëzman himself,
now covered in ridicule, was professionally ruined. Beaumarchais for his part judged it wise to absent himself. His talent
as a negotiator was known since he had undertaken a secret
mission on behalf of Louis XV. Louis XVI now entrusted him
with the task of returning to London to meet the Chevalier
d'Eon, a captain of the Dragoons who was posing as a woman.
The Chevalier d'Eon was a secret agent and most probably a
double agent, and Beaumarchais was to buy him off and secure
from him an undertaking to wear women's clothes for the rest of
his life. This *travestissement* may have suggested the *travestissement* of Chérubin in *Le Mariage de Figaro*, a young page whose
part is traditionally played by a girl. The story of the relationship between the Chevalier d'Eon and Beaumarchais, whom the
Chevalier d'Eon allegedly wished to marry, makes, however,
very strange reading to anyone unfamiliar with the ambiguities
of aristocratic life in the late eighteenth century.

    The story of Beaumarchais's involvement in politics, in the
raising of a fleet to aid the American insurgents, in a conflict
with the Comédiens Français that led to the foundation of the
Société des Auteurs Dramatiques and the acceptance of the

principle of an author's copyright, needs to be read in any of the biographies of Beaumarchais's life. He certainly remained under a cloud till he finally won his suit against La Blache (23 July 1776) and even then opinion was divided about the man, a fact which did not help him in his long struggle against the royal censors of his *Mariage*.

The briefest outline of Beaumarchais's activities in the years preceding the performance of his play serves to bring out that in addition to the publicity surrounding *Le Mariage*, he himself had been much in the public eye as a man involved in shady affairs and legal wrangles, and that he was a writer of uncommon audacity. In all the circles that mattered, at Court, among the aristocracy and the bourgeoisie, the men of finance and of law, theatre-goers and actors, he had achieved notoriety. Whether welcomed in the entourage of Choiseul or viewed with suspicion in that of Louis XVI, his actions always made news. With the intellectuals and the *philosophes* he was popular on account of his wit and his satire of current abuses; with the bourgeoisie his attack on the courts as corrupt and oppressive met with approval; in other circles he provided entertainment and gossip. The idea that *Le Mariage de Figaro* might reflect current events, and Figaro himself prove to be none other than a projection of the author himself, was present in most people's minds and doubtless contributed to the curiosity the play awakened. That the public flocked to see the play and that it was enjoyed in very different ways is not in doubt. The *Correspondance secrète* (12 May 1784 and 20 October 1784), the *Année littéraire* (IV, lettre 1, 1784), the *Mémoires secrets* (27 April, 1 May 1784), as well as the critical Fleury in his *Mémoires* and La Harpe in the *Correspondance littéraire*, testify to its overwhelming success. But of course it is only the immediate success of the play that can be explained in part by the circumstances attending its performance, and the life and activities of its author. For an explanation of its lasting success we must surely look elsewhere.

B. Contemporary Background

Attempts to present the play in modern dress have proved disappointing. Part of its charm lies in its presentation of eighteenth-century society, its manners, its costume, its colourful yet effete aristocracy with its loose moral values. We enjoy going back in time to the glittering period of rococo, to Madame de Pompadour and the ill-fated Marie Antoinette. The backcloth is like a tableau of Fragonard and there is a scene taken from a painting by Carle Van Loo. The silk sheen and fine lace of the dresses of the Comtesse which successfully replaced the more modest *lévite* requested by Beaumarchais and fashionable in 1780, the be-ribboned attire of the peasant girls and the extravagant dress of Figaro help to take us into a strange dreamlike world where values and terms of reference are very different from our own. We watch at first without being involved, but there is enough general humanity in the characters to give reality to their actions and make us respond. We feel at once *dépaysés* and at home, and our own drab world recedes from our consciousness to let us partake of a feast for the eyes, the ears and the mind.

When presented with *Le Mariage de Figaro*, as indeed with *Le Barbier de Séville*, we experience in some strange way the same kind of liberation as when confronted by a play by Marivaux in which the scene is situated in some never-never land or in some enchanted world of love. In spite of its Spanish trappings we situate the comedy in the France of the Ancien Régime of which it is an undoubted product, and instinctively endorse Jacques Vier's sub-title to his study of the work: *miroir d'un siècle, portrait d'un homme*. We are titillated by its alleged immorality, just as when viewing a Restoration comedy, or indeed *The Beggars' Opera*, that characteristic eighteenth-century work successfully revived throughout the century and to the present day. But need we then conclude that we appreciate the play for completely different reasons from those that moved Beaumarchais's contemporaries?

Surprisingly, we find that the audience in the eighteenth century was faced with a similar phenomenon. The spectator then was immediately aware of the Spanish setting which revived memories of Lesage and more generally of the Spanish influence so strong in the early part of the century before the English

influence became paramount. *Le Mariage de Figaro*, as first performed, was set in the same period as *Le Barbier de Séville*, that
is to say in the fifteenth century, the golden age of Queen
Isabella. The Spanish décor, dress and colour served to distance
the spectator from the events enacted on the stage in a way
Italian comedy had done and continued to do in Paris until
1762. The audience would feel the *dépaysement*, and experience
a sense of alienation from the characters which contemporary
references and thought could allay but not remove. The
costumes adopted were sumptuous but many would seem incongruous, and it should be noted that Beaumarchais himself
specified them with very great care and attention to detail,
presumably to heighten the overall effect, but also because he
saw the link between dress and character, a point his preliminary
note brings out and, incidentally, one which Bernard Shaw was
later to exploit. However appropriate the Spanish décor may be,
it was, however, manifestly bogus and recognised as a means of
disarming censorship, just as the oriental setting of Voltaire's
contes or indeed the Persian setting of Montesquieu's *Lettres
persanes* afforded these authors a measure of protection. In
Zadig Voltaire overemphasized the fact that the action takes
place in Babylon so that his readers should know for a certainty
that he meant Paris. These foreign settings ultimately failed to
deceive and served to make the public more aware of universal
traits sheltering behind national characteristics, thereby enhanc-
ing the social satire. Significantly, the styles adopted, ostensibly
that of the Spaniards of the time of Queen Isabella, were quickly
followed by ladies of fashion and what was anachronistic or
exotic became contemporary.

There is another factor which needs to be borne in mind. The
play, when transposed into its true French setting, records a way
of life, a pattern of aristocratic behaviour and relations between
the sexes, and between master and servant, that belonged to an
earlier period. Middle-aged men in the audience would enjoy the
humorous presentation of a life of pleasure and pursuit of
pleasure which turned around a conception of love that belonged
to their happier youth. They could appreciate the rumblings
of revolution and expressions of social transformation dis-

cernible in the play as they sensed that in art the world of rococo
was giving way to the harsher style of neo-classicism expressive
of a new and harsher mood, but they still longed for escape. *Le
Mariage*, despite its serious undertones, provided a door of
escape into a happy past. Even members of the pleasure-loving
aristocracy that did not foresee the coming *débâcle* took delight
in toying with revolutionary ideas, condemning abuses which
they would do nothing to remedy. Heavily in debt and yet pro-
fligate, they turned to the King for succour and to the theatre
and the novel for entertainment. Voltaire's *pistolets de poche*
had accustomed one and all to appreciate wit and satire of a
moral and social kind whether directly or indirectly expressed.
Gibes against the government as well as against the clergy were
the order of the day. The new *parlements* were far from popular
and increased the demand for judicial reform. Men were increasingly concerned over their rights. The world had indeed become
riotous before 1789 and the storming of the Bastille. The riotous
atmosphere of *Le Mariage* was a kind of mirror of a society with
which the spectator could identify. There remains something
piquant in a transposition of much contemporary thinking into
another country and an earlier period in time; and the spectator,
all unsuspecting, is in practice jostled by the strange context into
a new awareness of contemporary problems, the more so in that
he is constantly being diverted and amused. The man of the
eighteenth century as that of the twentieth, is thus at once
detached from the scene before him, eager to enjoy a *fête
galante* with all the tricks of slapstick and farce, and receptive to
the disturbing moral, political and social undertones which he is
pleased to detect. And if the play lends itself to the enchantment
of Mozart's music and finds its culmination in the gloaming
among the chestnut trees in a décor worthy of the *Embarque-
ment pour Cythère* by Watteau, no spectator could fail to note
the slaps as well as the kisses.

C. Eighteenth-Century Theatre

The eighteenth century offered an astonishing variety of comic
genres. There was the classical tradition inherited from Molière

which the Théâtre Français upheld. It contained elements of
farce derived from an older French tradition and other elements
borrowed from Italian comedy and comedy of manners, but it
was essentially a comedy of character. With Regnard, Dancourt,
Lesage and others, comedy of manners and social satire grew in
importance, whilst with Marivaux there sprung up a new theatre
of love more akin to the spirit of Watteau and the *fêtes galantes*
and essentially in the tradition of *commedia dell'arte*.
Characterisation gave way to the presentation of young lovers as
yet without marked personality outside their essentially adolescent but complex emotions. The slapstick of sheer farce now
took a back seat yielding to *intermèdes musicaux* and other
refinements.

It needs to be recalled that until 1762 if not 1765 the Italian
players who boasted some very fine actors played on the
Parisian stage, side by side with French comedies, improvised
scenes in Italian based on Italian *scenarii*, and that the spontaneity of their performance — with emphasis on expressive
gestures and facial expressions — exercised a lasting and
beneficial influence on the theatre and on the techniques of acting. One off-shoot were the *parades*, which were commonly
satirical in content, often improvised and usually scandalous,
which were first performed on fair-grounds, but in Beaumarchais's time in private theatres. Beaumarchais knew this type of
play well, and his natural facility found in it an outlet. We have
a number of his *parades*, including the one which marks the first
stage of *Le Barbier de Séville* (see *52*, pp.976-99 and *51*, pp.963-
75), whilst an *opera-buffa* marks the second.

In addition to writing scurrilous *parades* in a snappy, peculiar
style that survives on occasion in his plays, he was no mean
musician and improvised *vaudevilles* and other short pieces,
though he mostly adapted Spanish tunes brought back from
Madrid, or wrote new couplets on old tunes which he accompanied on the guitar. An interesting fact which has just recently
emerged from an examination of Beaumarchais's papers only
now available, is that whilst in Madrid Beaumarchais frequented
the theatre and enjoyed the *entremes*, close to the French

parades and the playlets or *saynètes*[6] of Ramón de la Cruz, certain features of which he adopted for *Le Barbier de Séville* and carried through to *Le Mariage*. At this time there was a determined effort to merge different genres. From this opera and ballet benefited, but so did the theatre. *Le Mariage de Figaro* includes songs, dances and music in the style of *opéra-comique*.

The characteristic genre of the latter half of the century is the *drame bourgeois*,[7] in part a development of the *comédie larmoyante* of Nivelle de la Chaussée. This new type of theatre offered a serious entertainment, neither tragedy, nor comedy, which held moral lessons. Characters were subordinated to situations and a new realism was born. No longer were kings and princes to dominate the stage, but ordinary people were to be presented in ordinary situations and family relations were to be stressed. Costume, tableaux and pithy repartees, soon to become proverbial, were to provide a new interest, as well as 'philosophical' propaganda heralding the advent of the new bourgeoisie. Diderot was the theorist of the *drame*, but Beaumarchais, in his *Essai sur le genre dramatique sérieux* which serves as a preface to *Eugénie*, developed Diderot's ideas which he endorsed and to which he clung even after the success of his two great comedies. *Eugénie* and *Les Deux Amis* are undoubtedly *drames* as is *La Mère coupable*, and even *Tarare* bears the stamp of the *drame* in so far as it purports to be a philosophical opera.

Now it has been asserted that in both *Le Barbier* and *Le Mariage* Beaumarchais returned to the mainspring of comedy: true laughter, and many have attempted to situate him in the tradition of Molière. In a sense this is justified for Beaumarchais's plays are true comedy and can be used as

---

[6] See Donvez (*47*). In 1764 Beaumarchais saw *El Barbero* by Don Ramón de la Cruz. This *saynète* may well have suggested to him the title of his *Le Barbier de Séville*. It contains a scene in which the barber draws up six marriage contracts, makes *pâtés*, and reads the same text twice over with a different meaning each time. Beaumarchais may have remembered this scene in *Le Mariage de Figaro*, III, 15, when writing the role of Double-Main. He is known to have seen this and other *saynètes*, as also Lemonnier's *Le Tuteur amoureux* performed by the talented company of Maria Ladvenant.

[7] See F. Gaiffe, *Le Drame en France au XVIIIe siècle*, Paris: A. Colin, 1910.

exemplars for theories of laughter. Yet the truth is more complex. It would indeed have been strange if nothing of his cherished dramatic theories had been retained. The serious tone, the social preoccupations, the feminism as expressed by Marceline, the moral consciousness in what some may consider an immoral play, are all there and fit in well with the contemporary *drames*, as does Figaro himself in so far as he is more than a valet as conceived by Molière and by Regnard, or the Harlequin of Italian comedy. For Beaumarchais the *drame* opened up new vistas which enabled him to cut across the stereotypes of the previous age and present his own characters with a freedom in keeping with his own deep aspirations. His chief characters do not quite exist in their own right as do those of Molière. Situations mould and change them, and they also reflect the moods of their creator.

So Beaumarchais has drawn on the tradition of farce whether French or Italian, of classical comedy and contemporary French and Spanish light comedy, mostly however on the *drame bourgeois*, as evidenced by the importance accorded to the plot, the costumes, the scenic effects, the tableaux and the social and philosophical *critique* — albeit in a new key, for the joyous note was missing from all the *drames*. There is, too, the influence of opera, as seen in the number of characters on stage, and the stress on music, dance and singing so obvious in *Le Mariage*. Far more superficial are the literary sources which critics have tried to pinpoint. Had not Nivelle de la Chaussée in *Le Préjugé à la mode* staged the character of the aristocratic libertine forsaking his lady yet showing jealousy? Are not recognition scenes to be found in la Chaussée's *Mélanide* and *L'Ecole des mères*? Is not a wrathful husband outwitted by his wife (II, 10-19) to be found in Sedaine's *La Gageure imprévue*? The last scene of *Le Mariage* when Almaviva puts his arms round the waist of his wife in the belief that she is someone else, and slaps are misdirected, may owe something to Molière's *George Dandin*, but perhaps also to Dufresny's *Le Double Veuvage* more surely than his *Rencontre imprévue*. Lintilhac refers to possible borrowings from Scarron's *La Précaution inutile*, Vadé's *Il était temps* and *Le Trompeur trompé* (which Beaumarchais saw in Seville), Favart's

Ninette à la cour, and Marivaux's *La Double Inconstance*, not to mention Racine's *Les Plaideurs* and Voltaire's *Le Droit du seigneur*. Vier has added Fagan's *Un Rendez-vous*, and Poinsinet's *Le Cercle* and *Le Jaloux sans amour*.

One may conclude that in the theatre there is very little that is absolutely original, but a close examination of these texts reveals dissimilarities more striking than the superficial likenesses. The most significant literary debt is to Rochon de Chabanne's *Heureusement* (1762), which Beaumarchais acknowledged somewhat playfully in his Preface. In it we find that Lindor, who resembles Chérubin, is loved by both a servant wench and her mistress, and comes close to placing the latter in a compromising situation whilst her husband is away. Forestier (see *11*, I, p.12) has suggested that Beaumarchais's visits to England and acquaintance with Shakespeare might have prompted him to mingle comic and tragic elements in his play and adopt a variety of tones, but one need look no further than the *drame* for these characteristics, and the concluding remarks of Figaro in his famous soliloquy in Act V can scarcely be construed as an echo of Hamlet's 'To be or not to be', however enlightening the parallel may seem.

It has plausibly been suggested that the plot of the play was taken from real life.[8] Aguas-Frescas where the action takes place would be in reality Chanteloup, the home of the Choiseul. Choiseul himself would be Almaviva, Petit Louis, nicknamed Lubin, would be Chérubin. In practice all these sources amount to very little. The plot and the situations are common-place, and biographical and historical background in a sense extraneous. The comedy rests on the art of the dramatist.

More important is the effort that has been made to situate Figaro, the kingpin of both plays, at the end of a long line of *valets de comédie* that goes further back than the valets of Molière's plays and owes much to the Harlequin of Italian com-

---

[8] See Jeanne d'Orliac, 'Les authentiques modèles du *Mariage de Figaro*', *Le Figaro*, 12 Nov. and 24 Dec. 1927; Jeanne d'Orliac, *La Vie merveilleuse d'un beau domaine français, Chanteloup*, Paris: Fourcade, 1929. See also J. Seebacher, 'Autour de Figaro: Beaumarchais, la famille de Choiseul et le financier Clavière', *Revue d'histoire littéraire de la France*, 62, 2, April-June 1962, pp.198-228.

edy. Beaumarchais no doubt remembered Marivaux's refined valets and especially a *tirade* by Trivelin in *La Fausse Suivante*, as also the coarser Carlin, the last Italian Harlequin on the Italian stage in Paris. The title of Lesage's comedy, *Crispin rival de son maître*, is significant of the enhanced status of the domestic. But all these earlier valets, who have their office in common, are different in character, sensibility and importance. It is not difficult to show that Figaro eclipses them all by his dominant role in the play, his personality and also his pronouncements. He is not only the rival of his master, but is superior in intelligence and experience of life. He has had a varied past as is made clear in both plays. He is given as a barber, no doubt because Beaumarchais saw a Spanish play of that title[9] and knew something of the many barbers then being staged in Spain whose picaresque adventures fascinated and whose excursions into medicine and veterinary science were obvious sources of amusement, but chiefly perhaps because Beaumarchais can portray him as 'faisant la barbe à tout le monde' (*Le Barbier*, I, 2), putting everyone in his place or, more colloquially, cocking a snook at the world. He has had many professions and is far more than a valet. In no other case has a stage character been more definitely identified with its author from the very beginning, thereby acquiring stature. Comparisons with other valets serve chiefly to bring out Beaumarchais's originality and creativity. Figaro remains the last *valet de comédie* of importance on the French stage. Theoreticians of the *drame* disapproved of the character which belonged to traditional theatre, and in the coming bourgeois society there would be no room for him. Already Figaro in *Le Mariage* has lost the subservience still to be detected in *Le Barbier*, in order to present his master with a challenge that is new. Not only is he at least the equal of all the other protagonists, but stands before us as a man, representative of humanity at large, far more significant than his actual station in

[9] J. Donvez (*47*) points out that El Barbero, who incidentally is dressed in a costume very like that of Figaro, belongs to the family of *pícaros*. On card 1455 he states that the *barbiers-pícaros* were very much men of the people (*pueblo muy pueblo*) and challenged the *petits-maîtres* whom they served. With Don Ramón de la Cruz 'les barbiers étaient de vrais *majos*'.

life would warrant, in terms of pre-revolutionary thinking. In the genesis of *Le Mariage de Figaro* the role of *Le Barbier de Séville* is of great significance.

D. *Le Barbier de Séville*

As Beaumarchais himself saw it *Le Mariage de Figaro* is the dénouement or *sixième acte* of *Le Barbier*. The earlier play was based on the well-worn plot of the *jeune premier* in love with the young maiden held behind bars by a jealous old guardian; he wins the day thanks to the help of his servant and the connivance of his beloved and her *camériste*. Thus youth and love triumph and the play ends with the happy marriage of Almaviva and Rosine. From the first, as stated in his *Lettre modérée*, Beaumarchais foresaw a sequel of greater complexity in which Figaro turns out to be the illegitimate son of doctor Bartholo and of Marceline, now old and serving as housekeeper to the doctor. Beaumarchais envisaged a dramatic scene of recognition between parents and child and the eventual marriage of the old woman and the doctor, in other words, a return to the typical *drames* of his day presented in the form of a parody, since the play had to remain gay. The artificiality of a woman wishing to marry a man and then discovering him to be her son thanks to a mark on his arm, turning her unrequited love into warm maternal feelings, and the former opponent Bartholo now being embraced as a father according to the theory that long-lost children automatically recognize and love their parents, is obvious, and its presentation can only be accepted as an ingredient of comedy. In his anxiety to promote the moral tenor of his play Beaumarchais overemphasised this facet and what was known as 'la voix du sang'. Spectators must, however, decide for themselves whether Beaumarchais is seriously returning to the style of *le drame*, as is evident in the later *La Mère coupable*, or indulging in irony.

Le Mariage is essentially the story of the love of Figaro and Suzanne being thwarted by the Count. This well-worn theme was given new life by turning Figaro and Suzanne into the heroes of the play, whilst the Count, having wearied of his wife, seeks gratification by attempting to seduce his wife's maid. Beaumarchais was faced with a serious problem, one which attends all writers who seek to provide sequels. His characters had to be recognisable, yet sufficiently different to interest, and any new theme had to be worked out with special skill in the light of the old. This problem had been faced before when he modified *Le Sacristain*, *intermède imité de l'espagnol*, which is an early draft of *Le Barbier*, in which the seducer, a married man, had the leading role and sought to seduce Rosine who was the wife of Bartholo. *Le Sacristain* was entertainment suitable for the Etioles's stage but not the Théâtre Français or even as a theme for the comic opera which preceded the play. Beaumarchais made the couples younger and toned down the immorality of the subject.

Now, in *Le Mariage*, he decided to show his characters three years later and in a new and intriguing situation. The spectators recognised their characters, but quickly noted the effect of age on the Count and the Countess. In itself this provided an indictment of the Count's behaviour. The Count disappointed his public whilst remaining true to type, but the forsaken Countess held its sympathy. The young aristocratic lover of *Le Barbier* has plausibly become a libertine with the natural distinction and manners of his caste and a certain regard for his wife. She languishes and yet preserves something of her love for her erring husband. There is change, but the evolution is acceptable and skilfully marked. This change in the situation, coupled with the ageing of the characters, helped to add a gravity and *mordant* which the first play lacked. Other characters can be recognised by their dress: Bartholo and Bazile, as Beaumarchais underlined, were to wear the same clothes as before since neither had changed in character. Bartholo, a cross between doctor Baloardo of Italian comedy and the *médico* of the Spanish *intermède*, and Bazile are now unexpectedly on the side of the Count, a fact which serves to alienate the Count still further from us. References to *Le Barbier* are numerous, especially in Act I (see scenes 3, 4, 8 etc.) and underline the connection. But Beaumarchais has taken care to introduce new characters: Suzanne takes over the role of *soubrette*, the necessary counterpart to Figaro as Columbine was to Harlequin; yet she is given a new freshness and turned into an appropriate partner of the extraordinary valet with whom she is to be married. And as *Le Barbier* ended with the marriage of the Count and Rosine, so *Le Mariage* will end with the wedding and triumph of Figaro and Suzanne.

Le Mariage, originally set in France, reverted to Spain. Aguas-Frescas is ostensibly close to Seville where the action of *Le Barbier* took place. It is manifest that *Le Barbier* is present in everyone's mind, and it will readily be appreciated that many past elements have gone to make the play as we know it. In fitting these elements into the gigantic jigsaw of his play, Beaumarchais modifies everything so that nothing remains pure. He relies on the memory of his spectators, cheats a little, plays with his characters and situations, even with his literary sources. He has links with his forerunners, yet sports with the traditions of the theatre, often using its devices ironically. We find ourselves at once in a world with terms of reference we know, and which are even underlined by the author, and yet in a new world where everything is surprisingly different and arresting, plot, characters, situation, even the social and political background, everything carried on the wave of dramatic movement and endless intrigue. *Le Mariage* does not move quite so fast as *Le Barbier*. There are scenes of considerable substance that are slow and gain from being interpolated into the quick-moving action; they add intensity and a new resonance which enhance the masterpiece.

Beaumarchais realised an uncommon *tour de force* which he was incapable of repeating when with *La Mère coupable*, the third play of his trilogy, he turned once more to *drame*. He had this third plot already in mind, and the evolution of some of his characters may throw some light on his intentions in *Le Mariage*. *La Mère coupable* is the Countess who has allowed herself to be seduced by Chérubin from whom she has an illegitimate son, Léon, whilst Chérubin, not unexpectedly grown into a *libertin*, has set off for the wars where he is killed. *Pitoyable* in both senses of the word, wrote the critics, but this sequel, which does not merit revival, presents the characters in a perspective that needs to be borne in mind, even if the playgoer today as in the eighteenth century may be forgiven for ignoring it.

3. The Play

A. The Plot and the Action

We do not know all the stages in the composition of the play. Ratermanis has provided us with the text of three manuscripts side by side with that of the first published edition, of the preface, of different versions of the *Préliminaire de lecture*, the *Programme du Mariage* and extracts from the *opéra comique* which was to constitute the last stage of the play. The stemma of the manuscripts preserved in the Bibliothèque Nationale, the archives of the family and the Comédie Française, is not immediately apparent. The manuscript in the Bibliothèque Nationale is a rough draft, although not the first, and the action is incoherent in places. There is an irrelevant passage which Beaumarchais struck out from this copy but which reappears in the other two manuscripts, only to be omitted in the first published edition. The manuscripts show hesitation over the character of Marceline which obviously presented him with some problems, and there are many differences in Act IV. Marceline's feminist outburst involved some restructuring. In the circumstances, and in view of the moving of whole scenes, it is surprising that the plot is as consistent as it is.

In its main lines the plot was outlined by Beaumarchais in his *Programme*. At one level it is very simple. The play presents Figaro's love for Suzanne and their joint wish to have their love consecrated by marriage. It is thwarted by the Count who should be giving them his blessing since he knows his past debt to Figaro, his duty to his wife and the obligations of his social position. Instead Count Almaviva, who has designs on Suzanne, thinks that if he provided her with a dowry he would be justified in exercising the *droit de seigneur*, an old feudal right which he himself had specifically renounced, by which a young girl living on his estate could be required to spend her wedding night with him. This ancient, barbaric right which had never been abrogated, but which had not been exercised for many a decade, had recently become the subject of a play by Voltaire — *Le Droit du seigneur* — who had chosen the theme to exemplify the absurdity of antiquated laws and to discredit the aristocracy. The interesting point is that in spite of the absurdity of the whole affair it appealed to the public, typifying as it did the shocking abuses of which the people were the victims. Beaumarchais uses this theme, but in a fanciful and improbable manner. The idea cannot be seriously entertained in the play, yet the theme itself and the talk around it does help to discredit the Count, making him look like some fossil of the past, an absurd figure of fun well cast in a comedy.

By focussing on one abuse Beaumarchais attacked the whole system of privileges of the *Ancien Régime*, and the very absurdity of the abuse he chose in its contemporary setting led spectators to draw inferences highly critical of the existing regime without exposing the author to official censure. In law through marriage Almaviva had forfeited any seigneurial rights he may have had, and it is interesting to note that, in spite of the lack of verisimilitude, the satire of the aristocracy holds so well on the stage. Suzanne, of course, warns her mistress and her lover of Almaviva's intentions, and they band together to thwart him. A rascally young page, Chérubin, a dubious cherub of thirteen, liked and indulged by everyone, constantly upsets his master's schemes and even at times works against his own interest and that of the Countess through his scatterbrain behaviour. The Count being far from stupid realises that he is being duped, but cannot prove it and cannot even see how his discomfiture is being contrived. His allies Bartholo, Bazile and Marceline are equally outwitted. He decides to take revenge by upholding Marceline's absurd pretension to marry Figaro. She had lent money to Figaro on the understanding that in the event of his being unable to repay he will marry her. Donning the robes of the Chief Justice of Andalusia the Count now sentences Figaro to honour his bond.

Tragedy descends upon Figaro as indeed upon the Jew in the *Merchant of Venice* when he is ordered to meet his obligation.

it not for fate Figaro would lose out for he has not a card play. Antonio by his expressed unwillingness to allow his niece to marry a man who has no known parents, leads Figaro to expatiate on the circumstances of his birth and, quite unexpectedly, it transpires that Figaro is the natural son of Marceline and of Bartholo. The Count's scheming is brought to nought. Marceline and Bartholo then decide to wed, but their marriage, as indeed that of Figaro and Suzanne, to which there is now no obstacle, has to be deferred owing to the inopportune arrival of Chérubin. Meanwhile the Countess, who still hopes to bring her erring husband back to his senses, plots to take Suzanne's place at an assignation the Count has made with her in the park. But Figaro, learning that Suzanne is about to meet the Count in a clandestine fashion, is both jealous and disillusioned, and hides in the garden to confound them. His rage abates when he finds out the ploy being used, and eventually he enters into the spirit of the scheme. Almaviva is unmasked; he throws himself on his knees, begging his wife's pardon, which is readily granted, and at long last Figaro can wed his betrothed.

This mere outline, which follows closely Beaumarchais's own account, leaves out many incidents and fails to indicate all the ploys and counterploys, ups and downs, comings and goings of the various scheming factions. Guy Michaud has provided a detailed scheme based on one of two thousand standard theatre plots enabling him to reproduce graphically the numerous actions as they revolve around the characters (see *18* and *10*, p.186). It may be as well to stick to Beaumarchais's five acts and within this framework study the scenes one after the other.

The story is simply a battle of wits between Figaro, Suzanne and the Countess on the one hand and the Count and his allies on the other, complicated by the intervention of Chérubin and others, incidents and accidents. The battle of wits between the principals is further confused by the army of secondary characters, Antonio, Fanchette, Gripe-Soleil, Brid'oison, peasants and village girls who bemuse the protagonists, enrich the spectacle, point the moral, and possibly the political significance of the play, without changing the main lines of the plot. Pomeau has found that the play is not well-constructed, especially when compared with *Le Barbier*, but we are inclined to subscribe to the view expressed by Forestier (*11*, p.17) that the allegedly independent and secondary actions are in fact off-shoots of a main stem which Beaumarchais failed to prune owing to his natural exuberance. I feel impelled to condone departures from classical purity of style as from verisimilitude, since *imbroglio* is the dominant characteristic of the play. The court scene and even the final scene, that of the wedding, could in fact be cut out as extraneous to the main theme and indeed Jean Meyer cut out the court scene from his film version of the play, as did Da Ponte in his libretto. But this digression, which offers a welcome caricature of judicial practice and has roots in Beaumarchais's own experiences of the courts, serves to make an important point in his social satire which strikes at the *noblesse de robe* as well as the aristocracy. The final wedding scene is also an *hors-d'œuvre* providing a charming conclusion to the work in the grounds of the estate, in the gloaming lit up by lanterns carried by the villagers as they dance. It marks also a triumph of an essentially rustic character, and the concluding *vaudeville*, highly satirical in content, brings together the various elements of the play.

After a brilliant if brief *mise en scène*, we have to ask ourselves: will Figaro be able to marry Suzanne or not? We are kept in suspense through the intervention of the Count who claims his *droit de seigneur*, and Marceline who threatens a lawsuit if he carries out his intention. Almaviva's infidelity naturally inclines the Countess to listen with half an ear to the advances of Chérubin who professes a sentimental attachment for her, whilst showing a more earthly regard for Suzanne and for Fanchette. At times Figaro takes the lead in evolving a scheme to foil his opponents, at others Suzanne and the Countess herself who finally sets the trap into which her husband will fall. Figaro is therefore less dominant than in *Le Barbier*, and, whilst he struggles as manfully as in the earlier play, he is more victim to circumstance. Beaumarchais seems to have learnt that superior wit alone does not necessarily ensure one's triumph. Figaro's relative weakness further endears him to the spectator, and the shifting of emphasis from him to the

Countess as arch-plotter, which weakens the linear development
of the plot, kindles the spectator's interest. In the end the three
protagonists involved in fighting the Count find themselves
united, albeit for somewhat different ends, but it is the bond
between Figaro and Suzanne that has the best chance of lasting
success.

If Act I sets the stage, Act II outlines the obstacle to the nup-
tials and the reasons for the delay. There are now two centres of
interest: the question of Figaro's marriage, and the position of
the Countess who has been forsaken by her husband and decides
to join forces with Figaro and Suzanne. Act III is a brilliant re-
enactment of a bogus court scene with all its ramifications.
Figaro confronts the Count who is none other than the Judge, in
an inequitable conflict heavily weighted against him. After some
grotesque clowning and an attempt to hide, Figaro is saved by a
mere accident: the revelation of his parentage. It involves the
satire of the legal system which requires him to produce a birth
certificate if he wishes to contract a legal marriage. The prompt
legitimising of Figaro reads like some parody of Beaumarchais's
own struggle to re-acquire his rights as citizen in order to marry
Mlle de Willermaulaz and legitimise his own daughter. The act
may be seen as an uncomfortable representation of legal pro-
cesses showered with derision, and also a parody of the *drame*
with its emphasis on family relations and of well-worn dramatic
devices such as scenes of recognition so convenient and wholly
arbitrary. Figaro turns out to be the illegitimate child of
Marceline and of Bartholo, the latter responding slowly to the
new situation. After much confusion and hilarity Bartholo
agrees to marry Marceline. It may be pointed out that there is
nothing here or later in the play to suggest that marriage is a
religious institution decreed by God as opposed to a mere civic
contract. No marriage ceremony is staged, only the trappings
and the festivities.

Act IV should bring the play to a close. It starts promisingly
with the preparation of the wedding, but unexpectedly Figaro is
led to believe that he has been betrayed on the strength of a note
from Suzanne addressed to the Count which he has picked up.
He nearly ruins the plan of the womenfolk, who have failed to

confide in him, by setting out to oppose his own wedding. He is no longer the supreme plotter who never puts a foot wrong. The women are scheming to induce the Count to meet his wife in the park under the chestnut trees whilst imagining that he is meeting Suzanne. Act V is full of surprises, and further recognition scenes. Unexpectedly Chérubin, who in the previous act had dressed up as a young girl and having offered flowers to the Countess and received a kiss from her had been sent off to the army for his pains, is to be found lurking in the grounds where Fanchette brings him some food. It is in this final act that we have the famous disquisition of Figaro on his destiny, which slows down the action but brings out the poignancy of the human situation. In the end, as in all conventional comedies, truth prevails, all masks are removed, and everyone is satisfied. The final scene of forgiveness, and the presentation of what Beaumarchais imagined to be the true attitudes of the sexes one to the other, has its dramatic effect, and all ends with dancing and song. Figaro has married his Suzanne, the Count is re-united with the Countesss, and Chérubin is paired off happily with Fanchette before being despatched to the army, where perchance he will learn some sense and grow up.

The variety of detail obscures the careful general construction. Forestier writes: 'Le premier acte est construit de façon symétrique, le deuxième selon une marche convergente, le troisième est linéaire, le quatrième suit un mouvement ascendant, puis descendant, le cinquième se déroule sur un rythme accéléré de va-et-vient' (see *11*, p.19), which is a sound assessment of the structure and movement of the work. Scherer has devoted much space to Beaumarchais's *dramaturgie*, but, however one may look at it, one must agree with Francisque Sarcey that 'c'est un monstre que le *Mariage de Figaro*'.[10] It is no doubt this monstrous quality that contributes to the hilarity of the play, as do the many gratuitous incidents that cut across the main action. There is the feminist tirade of Marceline (III, 16), dear to Beaumarchais but already cut out in the eighteenth century, the passage on 'Goddam' (III, 5, 1580-1600) originally intended for *Le Barbier*, and inserted no doubt because

[10] In *Quarante ans de théâtre*, Paris: Boisson, 1900-1902, II, p.335.

Beaumarchais thought it funny. Many scenes have only a tenuous connection with the plot, but the play as a whole is more than its plot. In Beaumarchais's conception interludes of music, dance and song, interruptions, digressions, momentary pauses afforded by soliloquies, and spectacular scenes like that of the court of law and the wedding have an important role. They provide essential *divertissements* as they did in Italian comedy, giving a character of spontaneity to the action and consequent vitality.

For the sake of liveliness the author cocks a snook at traditional conceptions of comedy and the logical development of a theme. He even defies logic. Thus, if in III, 8 the Count has seen through the scheming of Suzanne, how comes it that he accepts so readily the *billet* (IV, 9, 2415-32) which fixes their rendez-vous? In II, 22 the Count sends Grippe-Soleil and Bazile to bring back the peasant with a *billet*, but in IV, 10 there is no mention of this errand and the audience in which figure the *gens de siège* takes place in III, 15 in their absence, a point to which Beaumarchais himself has drawn attention. If at the beginning of Act IV (1, 2171-72) the marriage between Marceline and Bartholo has been arranged, how comes it that in scene 11, 2518 Figaro jumps for joy and says 'Donc à la fin j'aurai ma femme', though this particular inconsistency can be explained by reference to an earlier version in which at this point his marriage had not been determined? Ratermanis, among others, has listed other inconsistences (*3*, pp.21-22). In I, 4 he finds Marceline's stratagem fragile in view of Suzanne's coming of age (III, 4). He questions the role of Fanchette in I, 1 and asks when and where the Count proposed to buy Suzanne and protect Marceline as stated in II, 1, 635 and 659-60. How can the Countess have failed to know of the romance that has been sung (II, 4, 794-839)? How can Figaro be so much in the dark since he saw Chérubin (II, 20, 1263-64)? Of what danger does he warn the Count? How can one explain the credulity of the Count (IV, 9) in view of what he had learnt in III, 10-11? In III, 5, 1576 *et seq*. Figaro is delighted to be sent to London, but suddenly changes his mind. Why? For no other reason than that it enables Beaumarchais to interpolate his tirade 'Goddam' and make stringent comments on politics.

The court scene (III, 15), admittedly funny, is nothing but a mock trial. As the case is an *affaire domestique* it is one on which the Count would pronounce judgement on his own. There is therefore no need for Brid'oison, lawyers, judges who all remain silent whilst Figaro pleads his own case, contrary to the common practice of the law and accepted principles of jurisprudence. Furthermore, it is Bartholo who pleads for Marceline. All this is a travesty of legal procedure as Beaumarchais knew full well. Again, how can the Count identify Figaro with 'l'homme du cabinet' after the avowal of the Countess, confirmed by Chérubin (see IV, 5, 2338 and 6, 2372-76)? One must ask whether there were other stages in the composition of the play that made such matters logically explicable, and the characters more coherent.

The frequent lack of verismilitude did not escape Beaumarchais. He did remove a few glaring examples of inconsistency, but he seems to have taken some delight in piling up incongruities of one kind and another. Furthermore it is clear that, had the Countess given the money owed by Figaro and paid the ransom claimed, there would have been no serious obstacle to the marriage of Figaro and Suzanne and consequently no disclosures in respect of Figaro's birth. Beaumarchais is like a conjuror who unexpectedly produces a live rabbit out of his hat and it is only upon reflection that the attentive spectator or critic can see that he has been tricked. It is the sheer pace of the action and effrontery that carries the spectator along a preposterous course and suspends his disbelief. To amuse is Beaumarchais's aim and, in addition to continuous surprises, we have caricatures, parodies and various forms of satire to occupy the mind of the intelligent but unsuspecting spectator. Beaumarchais flaunts his indifference to mere technical competence and conventional realism. His vagaries find their justification in terms of theatre. He has pulled off a *tour de force* which leads the spectator to accept the absurd, partly because through it all he has conveyed a glimpse of an ultimate reality, a fund of humanity which his puppets are well designed to portray.

The scene, first set in France, was soon changed to Seville. Typically the unity of place is superficially respected whilst disregarded in practice. The action takes place in the château of Aguas-Frescas, but Beaumarchais changes the venue from act to act. We move from a partially furnished room with a vast arm-chair to a fine bedroom with a large four-poster and a raised platform which has many doors, then to the Count's room in all its glory with a portrait of the King, to a gallery lit up by splen-did candelabra, bedecked with flowers, jewellery and all the trappings of a *fête*, and finally to a clearing or glade lined by chestnut trees with two pavilions or kiosks glimpsed in the descending dusk, an ideal setting for a game of general post. We see the gardens, catch vistas of the countryside with a road leading to Seville, as the action progresses. On every occasion the location has been chosen with care, sometimes realistic, sometimes symbolical, sometimes befitting romantic assigna-tions or a festive occasion. There are hiding places as in a Feydeau farce, alcoves, armchairs designed for a childish game of hide and seek.

The unity of theme, too, has been respected and flouted. Officially all the action takes place in a day, from dawn to dusk. But what a 'folle journée'! It is only theoretically possible to en-compass all these events in a single day. The disregard for strict classical dramatic theory is evidence of a newly-acquired freedom opening up new possibilities and, above all, reflecting the claims for freedom made by the author himself and by his mouthpiece Figaro. But the plot and the setting, however interesting, do not in themselves make a masterpiece of the play.

B. *Characters*

Figaro, the chief protagonist, poses many problems, the first be-ing his name. It has been said that it is derived from Fi (for *fils*) Caron, Beaumarchais's family name. But the manuscript of the play gives us Figuaro, which may or may not be derived from a comedy *Les Aventures de Figuereau* (1712) the text of which has been lost. In any case the choice of such a resounding name was a happy one and Figaro has joined the small band of proper names which serve to characterise a type. He has as a background the long line of ancestors to be found in French farce, Italian comedy, the plays of Molière, of Marivaux, Lesage and in the *parades*, to which some would add the character of Panurge in Rabelais's great work. He has the same presence, costume, carriage and self-assurance as in *Le Barbier*. He is now thirty, but seems even younger than in the earlier play; 'le beau, le gai, l'aimable Figaro... jamais fâché, toujours en belle humeur, donnant le présent à la joie... sémillant, généreux' says Marceline in Act I, 4, 182-87. He is as clever in scheming as in *Le Barbier*, 'l'homme le plus dégourdi de sa nation', as Beaumarchais says in his preface. But he now requires help. In a sense he has grown older, for he is more disillusioned, and one can detect a new note of bitterness even before the soliloquy in Act V, 3. He has developed a social and political conscience which was only sketched in the earlier play.

His increased resourcefulness is not so much a sign of age as the result of his creator's increased personal experience of intrigue and machinations as evidenced in his *Mémoires*. Bartholo is now a less effective opponent. Figaro has to face the powerful, arrogant Comte and his inconsistent behaviour, but there are forces ranged on his side from Suzanne to the Comtesse. He has had many professions from that of barber and veterinary surgeon to that of writer and journalist. He is no longer a mere valet, but a top performer with the inner assurance of his own worth, but unaware that he is proving to be a 'soleil tournant [*Catherine wheel*] qui brûle, en jaillissant, les manchettes de tout le monde' as Beaumarchais defined him in his preface to the play (see *10*, p.36). A master-schemer — 'De l'intrigue et de l'argent; te voilà dans ta sphère' (I, 1, 66), says Suzanne — he is proud, impertinent, overbearing, daring, cunning, and a fine spinner of words. He can engage in sharp dialogue and spice slogans with wit. His language is essentially that of Beaumarchais. He has stepped down a little in the social scale but his personality remains untarnished. It is not inherently attractive as an expression of *esprit gaulois* and a kind of rogue. But what renders him *sympathique* is his honesty in love, his suffering at the hands of the great and his obvious authenticity. He has his own integrity which is that of Beaumarchais himself, however much it has been questioned. He never fights an unjust cause and has a depth of feeling unrecorded in farce. His bursts of cynicism are understandable. He is serious, a kind of 'philosophe plébéien' as Arnould called him, who would really like to establish his own order of nobility, that of *roturier*, to take the place of that founded on birth or purchased by wealth. One suspects that he is very close to Beaumarchais, who had acquired his own title of nobility but when times had changed spoke in favour of abolishing all titles. Beaumarchais can be seen as an opportunist, a born negotiator and man of affairs, a social reformer, but not as a political animal wedded to a political party. Figaro, like Beaumarchais, is an individualist bent on vindicating new rights, those of the individual. He seeks equality, by which is meant equality of opportunity and equality before the law.

What Arnould may have missed in his analysis of the character and what Forestier has mentioned but with inadequate stress, is that Figaro is the symbol of the free man, this by statement and inference in *Le Mariage* only a little less obviously than in *Le Barbier*. He has sometimes been turned into the mouthpiece of the Third Estate, but he is not really 'l'homme du peuple, le grand cœur révolutionnaire', as Michelet saw very clearly. The concept of the Third Estate suggests a class of men with whom one can fully identify, whilst Figaro embodies the basically anarchical man, recalcitrant in front of authority and bent on his own self-advancement. He may be the common man, but not the common man who would abdicate his selfish interest to merge consciously with the broad self-interest of a social class, even his own. As Gil Blas in Lesage's novel, Candide in Voltaire's philosophical tale or indeed the Neveu de Rameau in Diderot's satire, Figaro is an individual involved in a personal struggle for survival in a society with which he is in conflict. Figaro is the outsider, the bastard who has, however, a mark on his arm to prove his parentage, as ironically significant as the lineage of Cunégonde's brother so proudly proclaimed by him in *Candide*. Thanks to his marriage, Figaro will be able to reintegrate into society, although the institution of marriage is hardly strengthened by the comedy that precedes the wedding.

There is a depth in Figaro brought about by the collusion of
the Countess and Suzanne in a plot of which he is ignorant but
which comes in part from Beaumarchais's own experience of
life. Behind the stock character we see a man very much alone in
a world in which he needs to survive and make his destiny, consciously and unconsciously self-centred and finding an excuse
for his lack of scruples in the fundamentally immoral world
around him. Always well-aware of his personal advantage as
well as of the dangers he is running, resentful of injustice and
making the best of the situation in which he finds himself, whilst
taking calculated risks, he is in fact struggling to get free, to get
his own way in a world in which there are powers he refuses to
recognize which are bound to attempt to thwart him. In the last
analysis, he relies on his intelligence and wit to see him through.
At times a figure of fun indulging in well-worn *lazzi*, at others a
tender lover who can be jealous and sombre, a tentative social
reformer, he can be viewed as an incarnation of the author, but
also of the common man and above all perhaps of the man who
wishes to be free to assert his right to live according to his own
lights. A new dimension and a rich humanity has been added to
what at first sight is a mere stock character.

Count Almaviva, the Spanish Grandee of *Le Barbier*, is a *corregidor* holding a high position in the judiciary and a coming
ambassador. He is a libertine as are his fellow aristocrats in
France, 'à peu près comme les autres seigneurs de ce temps-là',
says Beaumarchais in his Preface. He is worse than the libertines
depicted in contemporary novels — such as Valmont in Laclos's
Les Liaisons dangereuses — in that he is a married man. He is
sensual, cruel, fickle and an authoritarian. At one stage
Beaumarchais thought of making him less brutal, but finally
decided on degrading him through his intimacy with the
gardener and making him cruder, prompt to take offence,
choleric and eager to use to the full the advantages which his
rank has given him. He has, however, preserved the manners
and speech of a gentleman and shows good breeding. There is
something sad in his pursuit of women and there is a streak of
pessimism in his make-up. He still loves his wife after his
fashion, insisting that his wife should be a paragon of virtue;

and he is capable of jealousy. But his feelings for his wife in no wise prevent him from seeking gratification elsewhere. He sees nothing strange in trying to seduce Suzanne and indeed the lowly Fanchette. He is ridiculous in the eyes of the aristocrats for pursuing women outside his caste, whilst he stands condemned in the eyes of the bourgeois as a typical example of a dissipated aristocrat abusing his power. He has lost the sympathy of the spectators without provoking their hatred as a man, but only as an incarnation of privilege and inhumanity. His ambiguous attitude to women owes something to Beaumarchais, and if it can be said that Figaro is Beaumarchais himself in certain important respects, it can also be said that Almaviva is drawn from Beaumarchais's personal experience. He is more complex than the traditional libertine and, unlike Don Juan, is not irredeemable. The force of Beaumarchais's satire is directed not against the man or his instincts, but against the social system that has thrown him up and rendered him undeservedly powerful.

The Countess has aged more than her husband. She is worse off than Rosine, held prisoner by Bartholo in *Le Barbier*. She is cloistered in the home of her husband whom she still loves and wishes to retain. Lonely and vulnerable, she dreads the passing years. She has dignity and shows discretion in her suffering. She is sensitive and sensual, yet deprived of emotional satisfaction. Saddened by disappointment, she languishes away in a situation which she finds intolerable. It is no wonder that she allows herself to be distracted by the calf love of Chérubin, her page. In the early manuscripts she shows a greater interest in him than is the case in the final draft. She does not want to yield him to her rival. She knows moments of anger and *dépit* which her words readily reveal. Beaumarchais, far from being explicit, became increasingly reticent, leaving the spectator to imagine what has merely been suggested. As Ratermanis has said, the character gains by losing its transparency. She is scarcely ridiculous or even comic. Guilty, yet excusable, she remains enigmatic. We alternate between sympathy for a forsaken woman and misgivings over her more than maternal feelings for her page. She is sentimental and forgiving, yet practical. She wakes up to play her part with some fire and shows intelligence, perspicacity and unsuspected moral qualities in her struggle to regain her husband. But she demonstrates that virtue is not enough to keep a husband, nor are warm feelings and even passion certain to provoke an adequate response in a partner. Even when baulked and emotionally betrayed, she cannot bring herself to be unfaithful to her husband, but her own infidelity is on the cards and is the likely response to an impossible situation — as *La Mère coupable* was to show, for in this sequel *la mère coupable* is none other than the Countess. In *Le Mariage* she is not as pale a character as has sometimes been made out, for she is not entirely virtuous. Life for her is a cross to bear and she forgives Almaviva a shade too readily, but in a manner that enhances her stature. She is never stupid, and arguably she is the most successful schemer in the play, outdoing Figaro himself in the end. There can be no doubt that Beaumarchais drew on his understanding of his wife in his presentation of the Countess. Throughout the play Rosine adds a note of elegance, refinement and charm.

Bartholo in *Le Mariage* has a very secondary role, and his presence has been somewhat contrived. He is older than in *Le Barbier*, more serious, embittered, but less prone to violence. The essentially unattractive *docteur* of the earlier play is now still the stock character of Italian comedy with an aquiline, prominent nose and a traditionally vast hat, but without a mask. Bazile, too, has the same clothes as in *Le Barbier* and a similarly odious role. He can hold his own even with Figaro (I, 11; IV, 10) and shows appropriate malice. He is a gifted musician and a crook thriving on blackmail and calumny. He would marry Marceline himself and would destroy Bartholo for money. The actor taking on the part needs to be a good mime, but the part itself is a minor one.

The new characters are interesting and well-drawn. There is first the charming, quick-witted, resourceful Suzanne, a perfect foil to her betrothed's harsher wit. At one time Beaumarchais thought of making her part more important than that of Figaro himself from both the moral and the comic standpoint. Her nature is open, she is wise, has her feet solidly on the ground, and is prompt to respond when her honour or her honesty is threatened. She is intelligent and capable of devastating irony, reminding one of the Lisette we find in Marivaux's *Le Jeu de l'amour et du hasard* but from *soubrette* she has graduated to *cameriste*, a far cry from the rascally Columbine of Italian comedy from which she springs and its sentimental offshoot. She remains *verdissante*, exercising her inalienable right to voice her own thoughts as does Toinette in *Le Bourgeois Gentilhomme* and other plays by Molière. In this play she upholds the general principle of personal freedom. Quick at repartee she is an adept at slapping, yet, as her like, in Marivaux's plays, she is well-mannered enough to be able to change places with her mistress in the final garden scene under the chestnut trees. Forestier sees her as an exemplar of the Rosine of *Le Barbier*. Certainly she loves Figaro truly and healthily, but she is a more liberated woman. In her case, as in that of the Countess with whom she forms a piquant contrast, there are ambiguities. Her feelings for Chérubin (II, 14, 1037 and II, 15) are disturbing, as are her comments in the scene in which Chérubin dresses up as a girl. She is well-suited to Figaro and one feels that both are intelligent and determined enough to make a success of their future marriage. The two couples, that of the masters and that of the servants, may speak more or less the same language. What stands out on a close examination are the differences in mentality between servants who are oppressed but sincere and masters who are only caught up in the endless game of love.

Chérubin is a new and unexpected character. From the original fourteen- to fifteen-year old adolescent, Beaumarchais brought his age down to thirteen, a very precocious thirteen even for the eighteenth century, if not for Beaumarchais. The part was originally played by a woman and Chérubin dresses up as a woman in Act IV. He must have the physique of a girl, yet be athletic enough to jump out of a window and play games, and plausibly be given a commission in the army. He is awakening to love and starting his sentimental education, but his sensuality is general and easily aroused. At times he behaves like a courtly lover, proud of receiving a kiss, the first to pick up the ribbon his lady throws, even seeking to provoke the Count into fighting a duel, at others he behaves like a common seducer. A libertine in embryo — his behaviour seems at times to parody that of the Count who is his rival — he is indulged by the womenfolk, who see him as a child who might be playing with dolls, were it not for the oncoming of puberty. Beaumarchais's comment on the character that he is 'ce que toute mère au fond du coeur voudrait peut-être que fût son fils, quoiqu'elle dût beaucoup en souffrir', must be seen as prompted by personal experience, but also no doubt, as Vier has suggested, as a reflection of an eighteenth-century conception of maternal love. This 'charmant polisson qui s'élance à la puberté' is in effect a 'grand petit vaurien'. He can distinguish between ideal love for the Countess and earthy feelings for Suzanne and for Fanchette. He is the 'mignon de son maître' (see *3*, p.18) as the contemporaries saw him. In the manuscripts Almaviva showed an interest in him but in the final version this turns to hate. He is indeed a projection of Almaviva's guilty conscience, and his misspent youth and general behaviour in *Le Mariage* are the natural prerequisite to the libertine he turns out to be in *La Mère coupable*.

But here in *Le Mariage* Beaumarchais has presented a moment in the evolution of the adolescent capable of awakening 'de l'intérêt... sans intérêt' as Beaumarchais put it. Herein lies his ambiguity and a key to his eroticism. His hold over the Countess is shown by the latter's obvious inhibitions, her melancholy and suppressed emotions. Her feelings are shown by the symbolism of the ribbon, as pointed out by Scherer (*8*, pp.143-45), first stolen by Chérubin after it had covered the Countess's bosom (II, 26, 1493), finally to become the garter of the bride which Chérubin takes back (V, 19, 3191-92). The Countess has given up his token of love and overcome temptation, but the symbolical exchange has taken place and the garter, now bespotted with blood, suggests possession. Green[11] thinks that the intrusion of Chérubin was a mistake since he is extraneous to the main plot, but in fact he adds a dimension to the play, providing a spicy immorality within an essential moral framework, serving more as a warning than as an example to be followed. His presence also

[11] F.C. Green, *Minuet: a critical survey of French and English literary ideas in the XVIIIth century*, London: Dent, 1935, p.190.

complicates the plot, for he thwarts accidentally the best laid schemes of one or other of the chief protagonists and enriches the psychological study through his special relationship with each of the other characters.

This portrayal of a precocious adolescent may owe something to Lindor in *Heureusement* and to the disturbing young page of Mme la Comtesse de Choiseul, as also to Beaumarchais's own youth as penned by Beaumarchais's adoring sisters who saw him as in love with women in general and all too readily indulged by them. *Cherubino di amore*, the angel of love, is in part a product of the unhealthy aristocratic society which Beaumarchais both loved and condemned and which was to perish with the French Revolution. It provides clear evidence of Beaumarchais's peculiar insight into realms of psychology very seldom presented on the stage, which are subtly disturbing. Chérubin's sexless sensuality, or desire without desire as some have defined it, is presented with undertones of foreboding that foreshadow his death in *La Mère coupable*. Charles Péguy in *Clio, dialogue de l'histoire et de l'âme païenne* (see *14*, pp.138-80) has contrasted the *romance* of Chérubin on the tune of *Malbrough* (II, 4) with the funereal song in Victor Hugo's *Les Châtiments*, and stressed the aura of death around a character that is by its very nature ephemeral. We cannot be greatly surprised when Count Almaviva pronounces his crushing epitaph: 'Un certain Léon d'Astrya, qui fut jadis mon page et que l'on nommait Chérubin'. Had he not died in the wars he would have grown up to become nothing more than a second Almaviva. In *Le Mariage*, however, he is a symbol of young love, Eros who cannot live in a world of necessary compromise if he wishes to be true to himself. With sentimental and romantic traits he is a child of nature who feels impelled to love everyone in sight. In its essence his is not the youth of people who can mature. He embodies eternal youth and a concept of free love that can live only in the theatre or in our dreams. His youth is 'la jeunesse de tout un peuple et la for-mule de la jeunesse de tout un monde, la formule de la jeunesse même absolument parlant', wrote Péguy (*14*, p.177), but although fascinating and innocent in his priapic essence, Chérubin soon becomes corrupt. Rather than to Eros of antiquity he may be likened to a cherub in a painting by Boucher or a gracious figurine of Sèvres porcelain. The little page is the symbol of a pleasure-loving century doomed to destruction, as is suggested by his later death. Yet in *Le Mariage* he helps to create an atmosphere of youthful optimism and an ambiguous charm which is the hallmark of this comedy.

Marceline, who is referred to as the former governess of Rosine but does not appear in *Le Barbier*, is now dressed as a Spanish *dueña* and is an immediate object of ridicule in her attempts to find a husband and gain status. In one variant Antonio proposes to her, but she shows her preference for the flashy, young Figaro who is so obviously unsuitable for her, and her desire to marry him against his will renders her ridiculous. She may in this respect be likened to the Chevalier d'Eon, on whose sex people had been betting since 1771 and who persistently sought to marry Beaumarchais whom he had met in 1775. In alliance with Bartholo she shows herself to be a thoroughly unpleasant woman with evil intentions, but her character changes suddenly and somewhat unconvincingly in the course of the action and she is shown to us as the victim of the many miseries of life, and as one who has been deprived of love. She assumes the mantle of mother with good grace by way of compromise. One of the villains of the piece, she now becomes a kind of moral heroine and as from Act III she stands out chiefly as the victim of an unjust society and an ardent feminist whose outbursts were too strong for the taste of the day and were suppressed, only to be restored by Beaumarchais in the printed edition of his play. Marceline's feminist tirades, in keeping with the spirit of the *drame*, and her presentation as 'la plus bonne des mères' are intended to win the spectators over to a character, otherwise too quickly transformed, by focussing attention on her ideas and away from her personality. Beaumarchais took her seriously and wished to avoid any caricature, but she remains an object of hilarity, and her moralising tone strikes a discordant note.

Fanchette is a precocious twelve year old, for she is not as ingenuous as one should like, and has already learnt to dissemble. She is naïve, though, and imagines she is in love with Chérubin.

Antonio, the gardener, is another character with more than one facet. He is a drunkard, yet shrewd, and he has the directness of men belonging to his class. He is simple enough to try to disentangle the web of mystifying events that have taken place, and he does succeed in unmasking Chérubin. More significantly, he holds his own against the Count and voices conventional morality by refusing to allow the marriage of his niece with a foundling, and by protecting the virtue of his daughter. In spite of what Beaumarchais thought there remains a certain moral ambiguity over his defence of traditional moral values in view of his personal mediocrity. This ambiguity only disappears if we think of Antonio in a political context as the spokesman of the lower classes. But his social message, if indeed it was intended, would not have been appreciated by the audience, certainly not by its aristocratic section, who saw chiefly a grotesque figure.

Don Guzman Brid'oison is an age-old caricature of a judge. He has a stammer to reinforce his stupidity. He owes part of his name to Rabelais's judge Bridoie and another to Goëzman whom Beaumarchais held up as a fool and constantly ridiculed. Other characters such as Double-Main, no doubt an employee in the Parlement with whom Beaumarchais had exchanged words, help to reinforce the satire of the legal profession. Frequently the stage is filled by colourful crowds of villagers and servants who animate the various ceremonies and in the trial scene provide a kind of jury. In the final scene they compete for our attention with garlanded young girls, musicians and dancers and, in a last whirl, they are caught up in a *ballet général* in which Bartholo, Bazile and Marceline also take part. We witness truly the 'branle-bas de la comédie humaine', to use the words of Diderot. But just before this spectacular conclusion, ten couplets are sung by the leading players, each preceded by the *ritournelle*. The words are in keeping with the characters and repay careful study, for they hold the key to the play in so far as it is a 'revue d'actualité déguisée en comédie'. This *vaudeville* conforms to the original definition of a light popular song of a satirical or topical nature and after *Le Mariage* such songs were interpolated in comedies with increasing frequency. Later the word *vaudeville* was used to define a type of comedy interspersed with song.

The characters as such have to be judged in terms of the play as a whole. However human they may be, they are stage characters, larger than life, Figaroics, to use the term Bernard Levin coined when introducing Mozart's opera. They have a common style and acquire a symbolical value of which spectators are aware. The characters offer enough continuity and enough change to hold our interest and show a deep humanity which owes something to Beaumarchais's own chameleon-like nature. They are likeable because they are at once fantastic, enigmatic and authentic. They acquire veracity through the network of relationships closely linked with the plot and structure of the play. They have been well drawn in their social condition in terms of the action but above all in terms of theatre. Good acting smoothes over transitions from one aspect of character to another, from one scene to the next, and minor inconsistencies even enhance the illusion of realism, for they often mirror the inconsistencies of real life.

C. *Political and Social Satire*

Le Mariage de Figaro has been viewed as a comedy of manners with a clear political content, yet Almaviva, the Spanish *corregidor*, would scarcely appear to the French nobility as a mirror of itself. The revolutionary intent has been veiled, but Louis XVI may well have been right in detecting its anti-establishment bias. Should *Le Mariage* then be listed among plays now labelled as *théâtre engagé*? The question has been persistently asked since the eighteenth century, and diversely answered. Grimm, in reviewing the play, referred to 'ce souffle vigoureux de la philosophie', and Danton went further declaring that 'Figaro a tué la noblesse', whilst Napoleon stated: 'Sous mon règne un tel homme eût été enfermé à Bicêtre. On eût crié à l'arbitraire, mais quel service c'eût été rendre à la société!'. Nineteenth-century critics and some twentieth-century critics have echoed these sentiments which, however, have been strongly challenged by commentators such as Lintilhac, Hallays, Scherer, Vier and many others.

Annie Ubersfeld (*8*) has stressed the ideological content, bringing out Beaumarchais's bitter tone in satirising a system rotten to the core. She believes that Figaro is 'l'unique person-nage du théâtre français qui reste l'interprète des humiliés', pick-ing up Hallays's words. Figaro is a 'héros revendicatif et populaire', and has become a type. His message, if somewhat limited, has kept its validity. He clamours for freedom, liberty of speech, liberty of the press and political equality, and manifests the revolt of intelligence against privilege, whether of birth or money. This last point is highly questionable, for Beaumarchais has consistently shown awareness of the growing power of money. 'L'argent, c'est le nerf de la guerre', has become a truism. Noticing Figaro's endless optimism, Annie Ubersfeld seizes on the right to happiness as an implication and as involving recourse to action. All victims of tyranny must henceforth band together against class oppression. The coalition of servants and peasants under the banner of Figaro at the end of Act V is seen as a revolutionary march. Writing from a Marx-ist standpoint, she accepts the idea propounded by Thiers that Figaro incarnated the Third Estate, and, by ridiculing the nobili-ty, undermined its very conscience to the point of making it laugh at its own folly and the very principles on which it rested. Does not *Le Mariage* point the way to the liquidation of the dominant class in favour of a new revolutionary class, more specifically the bourgeoisie? But this final step in her argument is surely anti-historical, for as yet the coming class structure was unknown, and contemporaries without foreknowledge could well be forgiven for enjoying barbed shafts aimed in desultory fashion which hardly added up to any firm ideology. There are useful slogans, much satire, calls for reform, and the language of indignation, but no political manifesto as such or call to revolution. Beaumarchais referred to the corruption of judges (III, 15, 1937), legal quarrels over trivial matters (III, 15), and the venality of offices, and he showed up the Count's verdict as a joke. He sees that one's fate may depend on an absurd deci-sion. He satirises the magistrature as stupid, formalistic, venal, pandering to the power of the great, 'indulgente aux grands, durs aux petits', but in so doing he is definitely in the long line of

French moralists and does not formulate a revolutionary challenge in favour of a 'justice de classe'. In practice he draws on his own experience, but this time, rather in the manner of Voltaire, he transcends the particular to indulge in propaganda that should lead to reforms, and this propaganda is no more than that of the *philosophes*. In *Le Mariage* Beaumarchais is capturing a mood and only incidentally sapping the law as one of the pillars of the state.

The attack on arbitrary power has often been underlined, most recently by F. Levy (*26*) in her interpretation of the play. There are certainly telling appeals for liberty in all its forms in the famous monologue of Act V. No-one had openly said that a man could be gaoled merely for holding opinions, and Beaumarchais's own arbitrary incarceration shocked public opinion without leading to a direct challenge to the system. But Beaumarchais's remarks hardly constitute a political programme. They reflect a general state of mind, suppressed feelings, a sense of outrage out of which the Revolution was born, but not the considered view of a political thinker. It may well be that it was because of this unsystematic approach that *Le Mariage* became effective as propaganda.

There are discreet anti-war outbursts (V, 12, 3079), more common in the suppressed passages in which the treatment of a soldier was compared unfavourably with that of a general. In I, 10, 563-69 one is reminded that officers belong to a privileged caste. The army career is branded as 'le plus noble des affreux métiers', and Figaro criticises the army and military discipline more in the text of the manuscripts than in the final draft. Beaumarchais criticises the pretensions of the nobles including the *droit de seigneur*. He makes a few gibes against the Church, perhaps less effectively than in *Le Barbier*. He mentions economic factors as determining the laxity in the behaviour of poor girls. More generally, he states that merit alone should determine status. There is nothing here that is new, except the tone which is striking and the rhetoric which is as telling today as in the early seventies. 'Parce que vous êtes un grand seigneur, vous vous croyez un grand génie...' Talent does not depend on caste. The message of liberty, equality and fraternity which subtends the work can still be heard today.

This is not to say that Beaumarchais's revolutionary fervour has not been exaggerated. He was never a political leader. He served the government well as a secret agent and in providing arms to the American insurgents in expectation of a reward. His role is that of an *éminence grise* pulling strings in the background and never losing sight of his own interest. He made strictures on the *Ancien Régime* because he suffered at its hands and even if one argues that a work may have an impact that goes beyond the intention of its author, it is surely far-fetched to say, as Annie Ubersfeld does, that '*Le Mariage de Figaro*, malgré son apparente légèreté, c'est pour l'Ancien Régime la trompette du Jugement dernier'. Scherer for his part believes that the content of the work is less progressive than has been thought, and that one should not look to the theatre for a political manifesto, which commonly makes tedious reading. But perhaps the very generality and superficiality of Beaumarchais's political concepts made them more readily acceptable. His ideas may be simple, even hackneyed, but their reiteration in resounding language gives them merit, and the cumulative effect of his slogans must not be minimized. Beaumarchais has made the essential point which was to be the *leitmotiv* of the Revolution: liberty, equality, fraternity. This meant for him an assertion of humanist values. In other respects he is essentially a *frondeur*.

If we turn to the social aspect of the play we have to ask ourselves how significant social satire is in the work as a whole. Some would give it pride of place. The mores of the previous decade have been conveniently encapsulated in spite of the Spanish trappings and the general disarray perceived. Libertinage in the aristocracy and among the officers was prevalent and portrayed in the novels of Laclos, Rétif de la Bretonne and Louvet. The decadence in moral values implicit in so many scenes points to the coming disintegration of society. The main symptom of change is no doubt to be found in the presentation of the love of two servants as the mainspring of the play. A decade earlier this would have been preposterous and the *outrecuidance* of servants successfully outwitting their master is matched only by the close personal relationship of the Countess and Suzanne. Shared apprehension and misery and a common purpose have brought the two women together. There is, too, between them, the bond of a feminism voiced by Marceline. This feminism, however, remains a useful backcloth more likely to arouse interest than understanding. In 1781, when Beaumarchais first read his play to the Comédiens Français, he was still moving a little too fast and it is most improbable that feminism or indeed any other social message was clearly seen as an important factor in the success of the play. Its function, as suggested earlier, was to render more acceptable the change in Marceline's character and role. The principles that should govern the relationship between the sexes, the rights of women, to which Beaumarchais would have been one of the first to subscribe, were matters for consideration at a later date. Beaumarchais has, however, the merit of being somewhat in advance of public opinion, standing in some no man's land between true enlightenment and surviving prejudice, whilst familiarising himself and his audience with a new outlook subtly initiated in the theatre by Marivaux and evolving equivocally, but unremittingly, throughout the last decades of the eighteenth century.

D. Moral Values

Beaumarchais was at pains to defend his play from the charge of immorality which was levelled against it from the start. In the preface to the first edition of the play he maintained that each important character, with the exception of Marceline, fulfils a moral purpose. In the line of all great moralists and of writers of comedy such as Molière, he claims that by presenting things as they are, and ridiculing vice, he both entertains and instructs. Has he not found the means to link comedy and morals by making you laugh with Figaro against Bartholo? There is a lesson to be derived from a fable of La Fontaine and any 'peinture de mœurs'. By depicting vices and abuses the playwright points the way to the eventual remedy, if at first sight, as in real life, they seem to triumph. Beaumarchais, however much he may have been a sinner, was personally an upholder of virtue, as a study of his *drames* would show, but he had to make people laugh. He exposes hypocrisy, and is not the final defeat of Almaviva essentially moral? Furthermore, the general plea for forgiveness is essentially Christian, and the Countess, by forgiving her sinning husband on his bended knee, showers her blessing on the bad as well as the good; but surely the bad have been taught a lesson, Almaviva is not beyond redemption. This tableau, however, which is worthy of a painting by Greuze, is too theatrical to ring true, and we remain convinced that Beaumarchais can have had few illusions about effectively changing man's character, as his sequel to the play made clear. But if one cannot easily change the nature of man, one may hope to change his behaviour. Beaumarchais made an important observation when he wrote in his preface[12] 'J'ai pensé, je pense encore qu'on n'obtient ni grand pathétique, ni profonde moralité, ni bon et vrai comique au théâtre sans des situations fortes et qui naissent toujours d'une disconvenance sociale dans le sujet qu'on veut traiter' (see *10*, p.25). By *disconvenance sociale* he means the contrast between the behaviour of a man and what one is entitled to expect from his status, as well as the obvious disparity between say Suzanne and the Count. The inner contradiction between the man and the mask is a powerful element of comedy, and it does imply a morality.

Yet from the first there were many who saw the play as showing 'la vertu opprimée et le vice triomphant'. Was it not a masterpiece of immorality and indecency? Did not a mere valet cynically deride a nobleman portrayed as a libertine, judges that were shown to be corrupt, and policemen of questionable integrity? And was not Beaumarchais himself completely without scruples? The critic and censor Suard, for instance, felt impelled to write:

[12] This preface is a polemical work written to defend the play against charges of immorality levelled by critics such as Suard who attempted to stop its publication after openly attacking the play in an address to the Académie Française. Beaumarchais had it published almost simultaneously in Paris and in Kehl, a town outside French jurisdiction, so as to defeat any attempts to prevent its appearing. It must have been written prior to Beaumarchais's incarceration at Saint-Lazare and consequent interruption in the performances of *Le Mariage de Figaro*, since Beaumarchais makes no allusion in it to these events. The preface contains significant statements which throw light on the playwright's dramatic theories.

Dans ce drame honteux, chaque acteur est un vice
Bien personnifié dans toute son horreur...
Quel bon ton, quelles mœurs cette intrigue rassemble!
Pour l'esprit de l'ouvrage, il est chez Brid'oison,
Et quant à Figaro, le drôle à son patron
Si scandaleusement ressemble!
Il est si frappant qu'il fait peur.
Mais pour voir, à la fois, tous les vices ensemble
Le parterre en chorus a demandé l'auteur.

The nineteenth century as a whole felt uncomfortable about Beaumarchais's moral values, and thought his ethics worthier of a *parade* than a serious play. Today the issue is dead. We no longer seek to underline moral values, preach a moral lesson and instruct the spectator in ethical principles. The morality of a play is as good as the audience, and one cannot foresee the moral effects of a play, for they will vary according to the individuals concerned. Under Beaumarchais's badinage, however, there is a morality: the right to freedom, personal dignity and happiness and to challenge an unjust and irrational order. But this right needs to be qualified. Society inspires certain necessary restraints which are well brought out at the end of the play. All must end happily in a comedy but the scene of reconciliation in Act V in effect forces the wicked Almaviva to bow before a social and moral order. Only the good can go free.

E. Comedy

Beaumarchais understood the requirements of comedy. He sought to make people laugh and not merely smile. He had recourse to all the tricks of farce: stage whispers and asides, misunderstandings sometimes based on mistaken identity, kisses and slaps that may go to the wrong address, *chassés croisés* or general post and forms of such games as hide and seek and blindman's buff, disjointed elements which converge in a headlong course thanks to the sheer pace of the action. Laughter commonly springs from the presentation of contrasts, often, as Bergson argued, from the shock experienced when faced with a mechanical movement which runs counter to our instinctive awareness of the smoothness and suppleness of nature. The final scene of the play for instance, enacted against a background of shade and light, needs to be regulated like clockwork, and the two kiosks or temples in the garden are like magical boxes out of which the conjuror draws whom he likes.

One source of comedy is derived from the presentation of simultaneous actions, the coincidence of events, conflict between people, incoherences in the pattern of behaviour or events, and also the inherent contradictions within a personality, ambiguities which, as we have seen, Beaumarchais was willing to exploit. The incongruous, the unexpected, as for instance when Suzanne takes the place of Chérubin, dramatic situations and dramatic irony can provoke laughter and reversals of fortune, and recognition scenes following on moments of suspense have for long been the stock in trade of the writer of comedy. The complexity of a plot accompanied by a quickening of tempo can lead to confusion and mystification. In Act V, 3, 2761-62 we read: 'on se débat: c'est vous, c'est lui, c'est moi, c'est toi; non, ce n'est pas nous: eh mais qui donc?'. The vivid, concrete form in which Figaro couches his state of mental chaos, makes us laugh whilst alerting us to the deeper meaning. The quick succession of contradictory or jarring statements or words can also provoke hilarity, as is found in countless dialogues in which repartee figures prominently; rapier-like ripostes have a mechanical and potentially comic element. The pun is another good example of the comic since it involves playing on different meanings or interpretations of a word in a given context, as indeed words that shock for one reason or another. If a character says something whilst meaning something else or speaks in ignorance without the inside knowledge vouchsafed the spectators, the audience will laugh. If Chérubin is hiding in an armchair and again in a closet and if, at the moment of discovery, the Count and/or the spectators are denied the expected revelation, the spectators will laugh, for they are facing a comic situation. The scene is even funnier if the Count shows himself as more stupid than is conceivable in real life. Laughter releases pent up emotions but there is often behind it a streak of cruelty which psychologists have noted. Beaumarchais indicated with great care entrances and exits, and in a mistaken effort at realism insisted on *jeux d'entr'actes*, by which the action could be continued during the intervals, albeit in a desultory manner. Time was too short to prepare effectively for the events that were to follow, and actors resisted this innovation for many reasons, but these *jeux* did throw emphasis on miming, and it needs to be pointed out that comedy is not necessarily or primarily verbal. A good mime in a comical situation will provoke mirth. When words are combined with movement, hilarity knows no bounds.

Comedy is not as a rule a suitable vehicle for philosophical disquisitions or soul-searching analyses which require time and reflection. Stage whispers, of course, so artificial when voicing the necessarily secret thoughts of a character, are essentially comic, and Beaumarchais knew how to use them. He showed originality in allowing Figaro to overhear bits of conversation whilst off-stage. When he worked up to the climax of the monologue by Figaro in Act V he was faced with a difficult problem. A close examination will show how he solved it and subordinated even cherished ideas to theatrical values. The monologue (V, 3), of course, is extraneous to the action and marks a pause in the fast-moving chain of events. It is a gratuitous piece of self-indulgence on the part of Figaro and on that of the author. Figaro's mood of bitterness springs from a misunderstanding, for he believes that he is being deceived by Suzanne. He lifts his mask of gaiety and the *être* takes over from the *paraître*. He recounts his life story, one which might have been penned but would normally never have been spoken before an audience whom the actors pretend not to know and at whom nevertheless they frequently stare. Indeed, it is by appealing to this theoretically non-existent public that Figaro seeks to justify himself and vindicate his personality. He is at once looking at himself and reliving his tragic life whilst justifying his actions and motivations in our eyes. He seeks our sympathy and wishes us to take side with him in the conflict with destiny in which he is involved.

His soliloquy is understandably rambling, singling out signifi-

cant details with appropriate clarity and sharp definition, yet it
has a shape and the unity of destiny seen in retrospect. It is
singularly dramatic in itself, and the overall effect is enhanced
by the vivid conjuring up of significant moments and through
imagery. The story is briefly but pungently told. Furthermore, in
this apparently long monologue, are to be found, interestingly
transposed, the elements of a dialogue of a most varied kind.
Figaro addresses Suzanne, speaks to himself, the public, the
world at large and, whilst he flits from theme to theme, retains
throughout a thread of logic which is his line of fate, one which
we need to assess alongside him. Take the opening lines 'O
femme! femme! femme! créature faible et décevante!' — clearly
this is rhetoric. He has in fact moved from the particular,
Suzanne, to the general, woman or women, and is in fact addressing all the women in the audience. He is trading on a prejudice which men condone and by which women feel instinctively flattered. Of course he is addressing the absent Suzanne, but
by assuming a characteristically French rhetoric, he is posing as
a moralist spouting some axiomatic verity. No-one feels insulted
or particularly enlightened, and both men and women are
delighted. So Beaumarchais presents us with the battle of the
sexes, the contrast between the ideal and the real, the misery of
life for a self-centred man who wants things his way whilst
knowing that between the fickle woman who deceives and the
male philanderer there is little to choose.

Figaro is, however, bent on a course from which he will not be
deflected, and opposition serves merely to strengthen his resolu-
tion; but he knows moments of defeat and discouragement. He
is trapped in his own brand of male psychology, as indeed is
Almaviva, and in a corresponding female psychology Suzanne
and the Countess. Figaro cannot change his nature and achieve
the detachment that would take him out of his despair. This
despair is new in this play and unexpected in a comedy. But then
so much that has happened has seemed fortuitous that we are
not surprised to learn that fate has taken a hand to prevent him
shaping the course he has planned. To carry us with him he tells
his life story in human fashion, elaborating on the first sketch to
be found in *Le Barbier*, I, 2. This story is punctuated not only by

flashes of wit and incisive comments, but by barbed shafts directed against his opponents and, as at the outset, by moving from an attack on a particular enemy to a satire of contemporary society as a whole. By sharing his viewpoint the spectator is led to identify with the man.

Vocabulary and imagery play their part in building up an effect that leaves one stunned. The choice of words proclaims the great writer. 'Je voyais de loin arriver l'affreux recors, la plume fichée dans sa perruque...' *Affreux recors* with its fricatives to be found again in *fichée*, the harsh rolling *r*s which linger in the ear, make one shudder even if the precise meaning of *recors* (a mere assistant to an usher who comes to seize pieces of property) is not immediately recalled. As so often with the French language, word order and inversion can enhance the vividness of the image. 'Sitôt je vois, du fond d'un fiacre, baisser pour moi le pont d'un château fort, à l'entrée duquel je laissai l'espérance et la liberté.' There is an evocative flutter even before one knows what is happening and hears the infinitive *baisser* so well separated from the main verb in the clause *je vois* and the direct object that is to follow. The time is the present and the presentation impersonal in that it is as if the *pont du château fort* has a power of its own. There is irony in *pour moi* stressed by its position in the sentence, for it is as if Figaro were some royal personage, and by the time we learn of the drawbridge of a castle we are all too aware of the true nature of the *fiacre*, and of the fortress that is to be his gaol. So words are skilfully used to convey more meaning and the change in the standard word order will tell the actor what he must stress. The dramatic quality of the scene is greatly enhanced by the style which, as in the case of Voltaire's, consists in saying one thing when you and your readers must know that you mean another — a technique that flatters the intelligence of the reader who has the pleasure of solving the conundrum.

It is no wonder that so many saw the key to the ultimate riddle of the play by equating Figaro with Beaumarchais. Have we not already been invited to move from the particular to the general? Why not now move from Figaro to *le véritable Figaro*, i.e. Beaumarchais, and then through him to Everyman? Are we not

one and all *roturiers* striving to better our lot and fight for our
own rights to the limits of our audacity and within the scope of
our brains? And does not Figaro's ultimate triumph involve *us*
and provide us with a kind of vicarious revenge on the con-
trariness of life? We too ask ourselves, as Hamlet had done, and
as Figaro now does, what is the purpose of a life we have entered
unwittingly and from which we shall depart unwillingly. But the
metaphysical question of human destiny is here resolved in practical terms by resort to action. There is more surprise than
anguish and the underlying optimistic tone, which is un-
mistakable, is well-suited for comedy, whilst deep pessimism is
the hallmark of tragedy. We respond to the call for freedom implied in a decision to act and the hope that it holds out. This
freedom, of course, can be very illusory and may lead to
trespassing on the freedom of others, hence the need to set out
the rights of man. Yet this essential freedom which Figaro
vindicates is one that cannot be taken from us. It is the freedom
to think and on the stage as in life this has to be translated into
freedom of speech. We revel in Figaro's unbridled address. In
Le Barbier, too, Figaro embodied freedom but in *Le Mariage* we
must note the limitations put on this freedom, which this
passage has underlined. There is no guarantee of success in the
mere affirmation of freedom, and chance as well as our fellow-
men will take a hand to cut across it, but faith that is the
characteristic of man and his struggle to realise himself is the
hallmark of his humanity, and in the end optimism triumphs.
Perhaps the ultimate message in a comedy conceived to delight
us was more significant than the definitely political message that
many have read into the play. The passage has magic. It verges
on tragedy but is funny in its incongruity and detail, and the
presentation is always highly dramatic. The call for freedom was
picked up at once and is still valid today. When in 1866 it was
decided to found in Paris a daily paper destined to become one
of the great dailies of France it was called *Le Figaro*. Non-
political at first it used the caption: 'Sans la liberté de blâmer il
n'est point d'éloge flatteur', a truism deftly worded by
Beaumarchais not in a treatise but in a remarkably dramatic
passage.

F. Language and Style

Does Beaumarchais's style hold the key to his genius? Yes, in the
sense that it is an integral part of his comedy and that it is fully
expressive of the man himself. There is a remarkable concord-
ance between the language used on the stage and the action and
characters. A great variety in language and tones does not
preclude a *unité de discours* which is the hallmark of
Beaumarchais the writer. The prevailing language is that of the
petits-maîtres which tends to level social conditions, but it would
be wrong to say, as has been suggested, that all characters with
the exception of the peasants speak like Beaumarchais. There
are differences in language between the characters and according
to mood or circumstance. In general the language is vivid and
colourful, sometimes naive and natural, sometimes clever and
contrived, sometimes rational, sometimes fanciful. The dialogue
is like the fencing of two equal sparring partners. *Reparties*
abound in verbal fireworks. There is insolence in the constant
persiflage and frequent parody. Beaumarchais has recourse to
witticisms and puns of all kinds, *double entendre* and twisted
proverbial sayings such as 'tant va la cruche à l'eau qu'à la fin...
elle s'emplit' (I, 11, 626-28). He juggles with words and sustains
comparisons with great verve, and may indeed be criticised for
indulging in too rich a vocabulary and being too ornate and
exuberant. He knows how to crack equivocal jokes, make in-
nuendoes and suggest indecency in unexceptionable language.
At times he falls back on the crude language of the *parades*, but
borrowings from all kinds of theatre, and even foreign expressions, are introduced and lost in the mad pace of the play which
Beaumarchais often forces.

He uses exclamation marks and interjections or expletives,
pregnant suspension marks, question marks and also sudden
pauses to enhance the effect. Beaumarchais knows how and
when to cut a speaker short, to move from dialogue to tirade, to
monologue according to the demands of the plot or the
character development. Above all he strives to convey excite-
ment and surprise by variations in tempo and speed of delivery.
Grammatical short cuts lead to sheer juxtaposition which in-

creases the pace of the action. Here is an example:

> Il faut ruser. Point de murmure à ton départ. Le manteau
> de voyage à l'épaule; arrange ouvertement ta trousse, et
> qu'on voie ton cheval à la grille; un temps de galop jusqu'à
> la ferme; reviens à pied par les derrières... (I, 11, 611-14)

Clear, vivid, this style is well-suited for drama. The language is
often associated with mime as in the following example:

> De bons soldats! morbleu! basanés, mal vêtus; un grand
> fusil bien lourd: tourne à droite, tourne à gauche, en
> avant, marche à la gloire... (I, 10, 566-68)

The miming which accompanies the words underlines the
sarcastic element which inevitably recalls the chapter in *Candide*
in which soldiers perform in the same mechanical manner and
adopt ridiculous postures. Mime is to be found everywhere, as
for instance when Suzanne mimics Chérubin and repeats his very
words in I, 7, 265, 273-74, and becomes a form of language in its
own right, providing nuances and subtleties which are missed on
a mere reading of the play.

The language shows an exuberance which Beaumarchais's
artistic taste and the censor's pencil did very little to check.
Enumerations worthy of Rabelais pile up in a crescendo; words
and expressions from other languages as well as dialect and
patois are to be found. Beaumarchais uses the Spanish *camariste*
for *camériste* in the list of characters, and of course *corregidor*
and *hidalgo* (III, 15, 1816), *alguazil* (IV, 9, 2407) and, in addition to allusions to *Le Barbier* (*Le Mariage*, III, 5) the Spanish
influence is shown in the *séguedilles*[13], the *fandangos* and the
stage setting of II, 4 which refers to Carle Van Loo's
Conversation espagnole (which should in fact read *Concert
espagnol*). In III, 5, 1667 we find an Italian proverb, *Tempo é
galant'uomo*, often given in French, *Le temps est galant*

[13] From the Beaumarchais documents published by Donvez (*47*) we learn that
when in Madrid Beaumarchais played *séguedilles* on his guitar, and was shocked
by the lascivious *fandangos* danced to the accompaniment of castanets.

homme, and in V, 8 the oath *demonio* (2988) and *Santa Barbara* (2996); *provero* (II, 21, 1359) for 'poor'. The expression *ques-à-quo* (V, 8, 2990), 'what is this?', is borrowed from the Provençal and already occurred in Beaumarchais's fourth *Mémoire* where it crowns a violently satirical passage against the censor, Marin, and had become so popular that it was used to denote a type of bonnet. It is deliberately used here by Figaro and repeated by Suzanne as she lashes out to amuse the spectator and win him over. *Pécaïre* (II, 20, 1265) for 'poor sinner', 'poor chap', is a term used in the south of France. *Tarare* (III, 18, 2145) is used as an expletive to convey disdain and derision. *A étripe-cheval* (V, 2, 3055) is colloquial for 'at great speed'. Peasants speak in incorrect language or in their dialect: *Jarni* (II, 21, 1305), *je renie Dieu*, is to be found as well as *pardieu* (IV, 5, 2313). Antonio's oath *palsambleu* (V, 16, 3135), 'by the blood of God', is in fact nothing more than a *juron de comédie* which shows that Beaumarchais is more concerned with theatrical effect than with realism. *Patouriau, troupiau* (II, 22, 1417, 1419) are also conventional, but help to create a rustic atmosphere.

Familiar expressions are frequent: *Ah! ouiche* for 'oh! no' (I, 8, 319), *me crottant*, *m'échinant* and *je l'enfile* (III, 5, 1659) for 'I deceive him', as well as *enfilé* (I, 10, 527), originally 'beaten at backgammon', hence 'taken in'. There are other contemporary references to words used for the game of backgammon: *Quelle école* (II, 17, 1123) which acquires the meaning of 'what a bloomer!' and to *pharaon* (V, 3, 2744), a game of chance not unlike baccara, deliberate corruption of words such as *balbucifier* for *balbutier* (III, 15, 1935), even anglicisms then fashionable. Beaumarchais knows how to be sanctimonious and even pompous when he has to make Marceline speak, how to give Double-Main a ridiculous stammer (III, 15), how to be meditative in a monologue that is in part a dialogue, how to be lyrical and well-nigh romantic (IV, 1, 2215-35) in a duo of love. *Ramassis d'expression* help to make the satire telling, whilst song and dance provide *divertissements*, often so dazzling as to distract from the serious content of the play, but not the comic dimension.

Beaumarchais claimed in his Preface to have adopted the

appropriate language for each character and aimed at a natural style. In fact his style is one that is eminently suitable for comedy and as such it can be claimed that it is a hotch-potch of many styles given unity through the flow of the author's pen. One element stands out: the *rythme endiablé*, so well suited to the *folle journée*, underlined by the number of scenes, and the picking up at the beginning of a scene of the words or actions at the end of the previous one. This movement, coupled with the repetition of a word or a sentence and indeed *coups de théâtre*, prevents the action from ever flagging and serves also to inhibit one's critical faculties and prevent any focussing of attention on unlikely events (IV, 11). The proper presentation of *Le Mariage de Figaro* requires a choreographer to regulate the respective movements of the characters on stage and the pace of the action as well as the dances and processions. The choreography, indicated by Beaumarchais, gives a sense of direction and unity to the work which the balance of costumes, specified with equal care in their diversity of shape and colour, serves to reinforce.[14]

---

[14] The manuscript of *Le Mariage de Figaro* housed in the Comédie Française, which may be a prompter's copy, has corrections in Beaumarchais's hand. It seems to have been emended in the course of rehearsals. The scenes have been timed. The position of the actors on the stage, and the precise moment when scenes have to be cut as actors come on or leave the stage, have been marked. Nothing was left to chance.

4. Significance

In the light of its manifold aspects, how should the play be interpreted? Is it the plot, the characters, the political message or perhaps the style that provides the key to its success? Every spectator will stress one element at the expense of the others, but many would accept that it is a combination of all the constituent elements in a true comedy that gives the work its meaning, and secures it a place in the history of the theatre. Certainly we may detect weaknesses in virtually every aspect of the play. We can challenge the originality of the plot, the very unity of the play, the consistency of the characters, the clarity and detail of the moral and political ideas conveyed, the purity of the style. This being so, we need to bear in mind that weaknesses can go hand in hand with great qualities in any final and overall assessment, and assuredly the whole can prove to be more than the sum of the component parts. Beaumarchais himself wrote in the *Lettre modérée* which serves as a preface to *Le Barbier de Séville*:

> Le genre d'une pièce, comme celui de toute autre action, dépend moins du fond des choses que des caractères qui les mettent en œuvre. On pourrait en dire autant de la qualité de l'œuvre et ajouter qu'il ne convient pas de trop dissocier les éléments constitutifs: sujet, action, caractères qui n'ont de valeur que dans la mesure où ils se greffent les uns sur les autres.

He was a past master in the art of weaving all strands together into a satisfying work of art, subordinating constituent elements to an overriding purpose: success on the stage. And conflict, ambiguities of all kinds, in subject and treatment, characters and style, inconsistencies and absurdities, problems of one sort or another are at the very heart of all theatre, which is first and foremost entertainment, and needs tension to come alive.

In our interpretation the core of the play is to be found in the presentation of love. We are faced with the game of love as in a comedy by Marivaux, but it is played with a difference, even if, as in all good comedies, the *couples bien assortis* triumph in the end. How complex is this presentation in *Le Mariage*? The straight course of true love based on a modern realism, sincere feelings and manifested in touches of lyricism but without any romanticism, is thwarted by the Count's weakness for women and also by Chérubin, an incarnation of the life force of nature at one level and a rascally putative libertine at another, who upsets the well-laid plans of both sides and significantly complicates the presentation of love by creating an atmosphere of *volupté*. The pursuit of pleasure as in some *fête galante* is transmuted into the more suspect rococo of a Mme de Pompadour; and side by side with the charming world of pleasure conjured up is the damaging world of seduction and corruption. L. Las Gourgues (*27*, pp.295-99) has suggested that it is the seduction intrigue that proves to be central to the play, overshadowing the marriage intrigue especially in Act III, and that retains the interest of the audience. *Le Mariage* evokes feelings of nostalgia as a last bouquet of a passing world which was closed and privileged. The sensual, suspect, yet attractive world of eighteenth-century love is what Mozart captured in his *Nozze di Figaro*, adding to the humanity already to be found in Beaumarchais's text a dimension of poetry that carries with it a spirituality which Beaumarchais shunned, preferring with the *philosophes* to divinise man on earth. But the love of Figaro and Suzanne has aspects that are unexpected in a comedy written by 1778 if not in a contemporary *drame*. The implied conception of marriage based on common sense recalls that depicted by Rousseau in *La Nouvelle Héloïse* when sanctifying the bourgeois pattern of married bliss offered by Julie and M. de Wolmar at Clarens. Suzanne, too, will no doubt become a 'bonne ménagère' and her marriage with Figaro, unlike that of the Countess with the Count, will know no cheating.

Against this background of love, new, hostile elements enter unexpectedly into the play, and the game of love has acquired philosophical, social and political undertones. Thus a new intellectual climate is created which Mozart had to play down at the request of the Emperor Franz Joseph, and also in view of the exigencies of music and the nature of his own genius. The political dimension of the play is very real and was obviously appreciated by Beaumarchais's contemporaries, as it is by many spectators today, but it needs to be seen in perspective. However greatly it may loom in our minds, it should be subordinated to the mainspring of the play which lies elsewhere. *Le Mariage* is not primarily a vehicle for propaganda and cannot be primarily enjoyed today for its political manifestations as such, but, by adding the political dimension, Beaumarchais was not only rendering his play topical but also enriching its fabric and adding significance to the presentation of the love relationship as he saw it. His political satire, both explicit and implicit and never didactic, is superimposed on a comedy of manners that is also a comedy of character which, from being lighthearted and frivolous, becomes the seat of antagonisms in which class distinctions have a part. Clowning around in and out of an armchair, fooling about in a *cabinet de toilette*, playing general post or blindman's buff, indulging in disguises, offering a *comédie ballet* with charming couplets must not blind us to the serious content of the work hidden behind its consistent gaiety. In the amalgam as we know it the very notion of genre disappears. Comedy of intrigue, comedy of manners accounting for 25 years of French history under the *Ancien Régime*, a comedy of love with two love stories at times bordering on the tragic, a psychological study presenting five characters in detail and a number of others happily sketched in, a satirical revue without real malice, with a political content but without a political theory — ultimately we are confronted by a personal kind of theatre, free from convention, conceived by a daring author, prepared to take risks and validating the liberties taken by his success.

By championing his own cause it so happens that he championed the cause of freedom, essentially that of the individual. Beaumarchais's last words, as found in an autograph manuscript in a private collection, read as follows:

Qu'étais-je donc? Je n'étais rien que moi, et moi tel que je
suis resté, libre au milieu des fers, serein dans les plus
grands dangers, faisant tête à tous les orages, paresseux
comme un âne et travaillant toujours, en butte à mille
calomnies, mais heureux dans mon intérieur, n'ayant
jamais été d'aucune coterie, ni littéraire, ni politique, ni
mystique, n'ayant fait la cour à personne, et partant
repoussé de tous, n'étant membre d'aucun parti et surtout
ne voulant rien être, par qui pourrais-je être porté? Je ne
veux l'être par personne.[15]

As an individualist bent on preserving his independence,
Beaumarchais was an outsider, but with little in common with
the outsider as depicted in existentialist writings, for he par-
ticipated actively in human affairs whilst recognising no other
interest than his own of which he intended to remain the sole
judge. Naturally he has been accused of opportunism and *ar-
rivisme*, when he was at heart an anarchist struggling for survival in the jungle of life with little else than his intelligence and
wit to see him through, and often feeling like a pawn in the
hands of unscrupulous men wielding unwarranted power. He
was gay in adversity and had the wisdom not to ponder long over
misfortune, or indeed question too deeply the purpose of life on
earth. He was content to free himself from prejudice as far as
possible and to deride absurdity as he found it. His chameleon-
like nature precluded him from probing too far into the arcana
of his complex ego. Instead he allowed himself to be caught up
in the merry-go-round of existence and to project his ambiguities
into his two great plays. Like Voltaire he shut his mind to useless
metaphysical or political considerations, and like him he pitted
himself feverishly against all obstacles in his path to self-
fulfilment. These obstacles happened to be the abuses from
which others suffered, so the spectators had no difficulty in ex-
periencing a sense of solidarity with him. His latent anarchy and
his unavowed immorality were kept in check by moral and
philosophical notions which made him realise the need to live in

[15] From a manuscript in a private collection. See *28*, II, p.539; *29*, p.133; *46*,
p.334.

consort with his fellow men. An epicurean by nature, he found himself constrained by the circumstances of his life and his desire to live richly in the society of men. Yet *Le Mariage de Figaro* has benefited from the secret conflict between what Beaumarchais really was and what he thought, a conflict unknowingly shared by his contemporaries. As other critics have done, Pomeau concludes his study of Beaumarchais by finding in the man himself the real key to the play. This is no doubt true, but it needs to be said that in *Le Mariage*, as in *Le Barbier*, although Beaumarchais has given something of himself to all his characters, it is not the whole man that we see portrayed, but the lively, stylised part of himself with which alone posterity is concerned, and which found its perfect expression in the theatre. *Le Mariage de Figaro, miroir d'un siècle, portrait d'un homme*, rightly said Jacques Vier, but it remains for us to fathom the work both as the mirror of at least a quarter of a century and as a portrait of a singularly complex man.

Bibliography

Brian N. Morton and Donald C. Spinelli. *Beaumarchais: A Bibliography* (Ann Arbor, Michigan: The Olivia and Hill Press, 1988). A well-nigh exhaustive bibliography with 2058 entries. For references to more recent editions and critical studies of Beaumarchais's works, see the annual volumes of *The Year's Work in Modern Language Studies*.

A. THE TEXT

1. *La Folle Journée ou Le Mariage de Figaro, comédie en cinq actes et en prose*, par M. de Beaumarchais, représentée pour la première fois par les Comédiens Français ordinaires du Roi le 27 avril 1784. Au Palais Royal, chez Ruault, Libraire, près le Théâtre, No 216, MDCC.LXXXV.
   This is the first edition, with an *achevé d'imprimer* dated 28 February 1785; it contains the *Préface*. To avoid suppression by the authorities, Beaumarchais had a facsimile of this *editio princeps* printed at Kehl at about the same time. According to Gérard Kahn, cited in *13*, p.140, there were some sixty pirate editions in 1785 alone. The first edition does not provide details of the music used in performances. These are to be found in some of the pirate editions, some of which seem to have notes by Beaumarchais, and in the *Journal de harpe par les meilleurs maîtres* (Paris, 1784) which may be consulted in the music section of the Bibliothèque Nationale, Paris.
2. *Théâtre complet de Beaumarchais,* édition de G. d'Heyli et F. de Marescot, 4 vols (Paris: Académie des Bibliophiles, 1869-1871).
   A critical, but dated and incomplete edition.
3. *Le Mariage de Figaro,* édition de J.B. Ratermanis (Geneva: Institut Voltaire, Studies on Voltaire and the Eighteenth Century, 63, 1968).
   This edition provides the text with the variants of the manuscripts. See R. Niklaus, 'Beaumarchais: *Le Mariage de Figaro*', *Romanic Review,* 1970, 61, no.2, 246-49.
4. *Théâtre complet, Lettres relatives à son théâtre,* édition de M. Allem (Paris: Gallimard, Bibl. de la Pléiade, 1934). Reprinted in 1964 with the *parades*, ed. by M. Allem and P. Courant, and again in 1973.
5. *Le Mariage de Figaro,* ed. by E.J. Arnould (Oxford: Blackwell, 1952). In Blackwell's French Texts.

6. *Le Mariage de Figaro*, ed. by Louis Allen (London: Harrap, 1952). In Harrap's French Classics.
7. *Théâtre*, chronologie et préface par R. Pomeau (Paris: Garnier-Flammarion, 1965). Includes the trilogy of plays with the character of Figaro.
8. *Le Mariage de Figaro*, édition par Annie Ubersfeld (Paris: Editions Sociales, Les Classiques du Peuple, 1956, many reprintings, especially that of 1968).
9. *Le Mariage de Figaro*, édition avec analyse dramaturgique par Jacques Scherer (Paris: SEDES, 1966).
10. *Le Mariage de Figaro*, édition par Pol Gaillard (Paris: Bordas, 1964, reprinted 1977). In Univers des Lettres.
11. *Le Mariage de Figaro*, édition par Louis Forestier (Paris: Larousse, 1966, 2 vols). In Nouveaux Classiques Larousse. Reprinted 1971.
12. *Le Mariage de Figaro*, édition par Madame Claude Hubert (Paris: Hachette, 1976, reprinted 1980). In Nouveaux Classiques Illustrés, Hachette.
13. *Théâtre*, édition de J.-P. de Beaumarchais (Paris: Garnier, 1980). The volume contains *Le Sacristain, Le Barbier de Séville, Le Mariage de Figaro* and *La Mère coupable*.

The text in its entirety has been recorded on tape and on discs by L'Encyclopédie Sonore, Hachette.

The Comédie Française has made available a film of the play (Société Cinédis) and a recording (Pathé DTX 303/05, Production Sonore Hachette, Collection Vie du Théâtre). The production is by Jean Meyer, who himself took the part of Bazile.

There is too a television film produced for ORTF by Marcel Bluwal in 1961, and there was another presentation by M. Bluwal in 1965.

The Comédie Française performed the play in 1977; illustrations of this production have been reproduced in a Bordas reprint.

On the production of the play by A. Vitez in 1989, see *Comédie-Française*, 174, March 1989 and 15 April 1989.

Attention may be drawn to *La Règle du jeu,* by Jean Renoir, the film which many have thought comes closest to the play by Beaumarchais.

Professor P.M. Thody has recorded a commentary in English on *Le Mariage de Figaro* for Exeter Tapes (no. F776), obtainable from the University of Exeter.

William Gaskill has published a translation in English in *Landmarks of French Classical Drama,* ed. by David Bradby (London: Methuen, 1991).

B. STUDIES ON 'LE MARIAGE DE FIGARO'

14. Charles Péguy. *Etude sur la chanson de Chérubin* in *Clio* (Paris:
     Gallimard, 1932). Included in his *Œuvres en prose, 1909-1914* (Paris:
     Gallimard, Bibl. de la Pléiade, 1957), pp.138-80.

15. F. Gaiffe. *Le Mariage de Figaro* (Amiens: Malfère, Coll. Les Grands
     Evénements Littéraires, 1928; reprinted Paris: Nizet, 1939). See also
     Le Mariage de Figaro (Paris: Guillon, Coll. Les Cours de Facultés,
     1930).

16. R. Jasinski. *Le Mariage de Figaro* (Paris: Cours de Lettres, 1948).

17. R. Pons. 'Le monologue de Figaro, explication', *L'Information
     Littéraire*, mai-juin 1951.

18. G. Michaud. 'L'Intrigue et les ressorts du comique dans *Le Mariage
     de Figaro*' in *Mélanges Souriau* (Paris: Nizet, 1952), pp.189-203. See
     also E. Souriau. *Les 200,000 situations dramatiques* (Paris:
     Flammarion, 1950); and G. Michaud. *L'Œuvre et ses techniques*
     (Paris: Nizet, 1963).

19. Jean Meyer. *Le Mariage de Figaro ou La Folle Journée: mise en
     scène et commentaires* (Paris: Editions du Seuil, 1953).

20. Jacques Vier. *Le Mariage de Figaro, miroir d'un siècle, portrait d'un
     homme* (Paris: Minard, Archives des Lettres Modernes, 6, 1957); and
     *Le Mariage de Figaro II. Le mouvement dramatique et l'esprit du
     Mariage à La Mère coupable* (Paris: Minard, Archives des Lettres
     Modernes, 39, 1961).

21. A.R. Pugh. *Beaumarchais: Le Mariage de Figaro, an interpretation*
     (London: Macmillan, French Critical Commentaries series, 1968).

22. C. Vincenot. 'Mensonge, erreur et vérité dans *Le Mariage de Figaro*',
     Revue des Sciences Humaines, April 1969, 219-27.

23. J. Ehrard. 'La société du *Mariage de Figaro*' in *Mélanges J. Fabre*
     (Paris: Klincksieck, 1974), pp.169-80.

24. W.D. Howarth. 'The recognition scene in *Le Mariage de Figaro*',
     Modern Language Review, April 1969, 301-11.

25. P. Rétat. 'La mort de Chérubin', *Revue d'Histoire Littéraire de la
     France,* 74 (1974), 1000-09.

26. Francine Levy. *Le Mariage de Figaro: essai d'interprétation* (Oxford:
     Voltaire Foundation, Studies on Voltaire and the Eighteenth Century,
     173, 1978).

27. L. Las Gourgues. '*Le Mariage de Figaro*, characters, intrigue and
     structure', *Australian Journal of French Studies*, 16 (1979), 295-99.

Bibliography

75

C. GENERAL STUDIES ON BEAUMARCHAIS

28. L. de Loménie. *Beaumarchais et son temps*, 2 vols (Paris: Michel Lévy, 1856, reprinted C. Lévy, 1873, revised edition 1880). Translated into English by H.S. Edwards, 4 vols, 1856.

29. E. Lintilhac. *Beaumarchais et ses oeuvres* (Paris: Hachette, 1887).

30. —. *Histoire générale du théâtre en France* (Paris: Flammarion, 1904-1909), Vol. IV, pp.391-471.

31. A. Hallays. *Beaumarchais* (Paris: Hachette, Coll. Les Grands Ecrivains Français, 1897, 4th edition, 1928).

32. P. Richard. *La Vie privée de Beaumarchais* (Paris: Hachette, 1951).

33. J. Scherer. *La Dramaturgie de Beaumarchais* (Paris: Nizet, 1954, 2nd edition, 1980).

34. Gunnar von Proschwitz. *Introduction à l'étude du vocabulaire de Beaumarchais* (Stockholm: Almqvist & Wiksell, and Paris: Nizet, 1956).

35. M. Politzer. *Beaumarchais, le père de Figaro* (Paris: La Colombe, 1957).

36. P. Van Tieghem. *Beaumarchais par lui-même* (Paris: Editions du Seuil, 1960; 2nd ed. 1978).

37. J.B. Ratermanis and W.R. Irwin. *The Comic Style of Beaumarchais* (New York, Greenwood Press, 1961).

38. R. Pomeau. *Beaumarchais, l'homme et l'oeuvre* (Paris: Hatier, 1956, revised 1962, reprinted 1967).

39. C. Cox. *The real Figaro: the extraordinary career of Caron de Beaumarchais* (London: Longman, 1962).

40. *Beaumarchais*. Catalogue of an exhibition held at the Bibliothèque Nationale, Paris, 1966.

41. B. Faÿ. *Beaumarchais ou les fredaines de Figaro* (Paris: Perrin, 1971).

42. J. Proust. 'Beaumarchais et Mozart: une mise au point', *Studi Francesi*, 46 (1972), 34-45. Beaumarchais provided a French text, only recently discovered, for Mozart's opera *Le Nozze di Figaro*. It is in many respects preferable to the later libretto by Lorenzo Da Ponte.

43. *Europe*, 528 (April 1973). A special number devoted to Beaumarchais.

44. *Missions et démarches de la critique: mélanges offerts au professeur J.A. Vier* (Paris: Klincksieck, 1973). Includes R. Niklaus, 'Beaumarchais et le drame', pp.591-99 and Janette Gatty, 'Du triomphe de Figaro à la disgrâce de Beaumarchais ou les déboires d'un auteur dramatique', pp.529-39.

45. M. Descotes. *Les Grands Rôles du théâtre de Beaumarchais* (Paris: P.U.F., 1974).

46. Janette C. Gatty. *Beaumarchais sous la Révolution* (Leiden: E.J. Brill, 1976).

76 *Le Mariage de Figaro*

47. Jacques Donvez. *La Politique de Beaumarchais* (Univ. de Paris IX, 1980). 1,947 microcards (a set is housed in the library of the University of Exeter).

D. *STUDIES ON 'LE BARBIER DE SEVILLE' AS A BACKGROUND TO 'LE MARIAGE DE FIGARO'*

48. E.J. Arnould. *La Genèse du 'Barbier de Séville'* (Dublin: Dublin University Press and Paris: Minard, 1965).
49. R. Niklaus. 'La genèse du Barbier de Séville' in Studies on Voltaire and the Eighteenth Century, 57 (Geneva: Institut Voltaire, 1967), 1081-95.
50. —. *Beaumarchais: 'Le Barbier de Séville'* (London: Edward Arnold, Studies in French Literature, 13, 1968, reprinted 1972 and 1978).
51. R. Pomeau. *'Le Barbier de Séville:* de l'intermède à la comédie', *Revue d'Histoire Littéraire de la France*, 74 (nov.-déc. 1974), 963-75.
52. J.-P. de Beaumarchais. 'Un inédit de Beaumarchais: *Le Sacristain'*, *Revue d'Histoire Littéraire de la France*, 74 (nov.-déc. 1974), 976-99.
53. J. Scherer. 'La scène de stupéfaction du *Barbier de Séville*' in *Studies in the French eighteenth century presented to John Lough* (Durham: University of Durham, 1978). Also to be found in the 1980 edition of *33*.

Bibliographical supplement

A. THE TEXT

54. *Beaumarchais: Œuvres*, édition de P. Larthomas (Paris: Gallimard, Bibl. de la Pléiade, 1988).
55. *Le Mariage de Figaro*, édition de Giovanna Trisolini (Paris: Le Livre de Poche, 1989).
56. *Le Mariage de Figaro*, édition par Bernard Combeaud (Paris: Hachette, 1991). In Classiques Hachette.
57. *Le Mariage de Figaro*, édition par Jean Goldzink (Paris: Larousse, 1992). In Classiques Larousse.
58. *Le Mariage de Figaro*, ed. Malcolm Cook (Bristol: Bristol Classical Press, 1992).

B. STUDIES ON 'LE MARIAGE DE FIGARO'

59. V.G. Mylne. 'Le Droit du Seigneur in *Le Mariage de Figaro*', *French Studies Bulletin*, no. 11 (summer 1984), 3-5.
60. 'Beaumarchais, Le Mariage de Figaro'. *Revue d'Histoire Littéraire de la France*, sept.-oct. 1984, 84e année, no.5 (Paris: A. Colin).

61. P.-L. Assoun et al. *Analyses et réflexions sur Beaumarchais, Le Mariage de Figaro* (Paris: Editions Marketing, Coll. Ellipses 1985).
62. A. Villani. *Lectures de 'Le Mariage de Figaro' de Beaumarchais: l'ordre social* (Paris: Belin, 1985).
63. Marie-Françoise Lemonnier-Delpy. *Nouvelle étude thématique sur 'Le Mariage de Figaro' de Beaumarchais* (Paris: SEDES, 1987).
64. Walter E. Rex. 'The Mariage of Figaro: a. Games; b. The monologue' in *The Attraction of the Contrary, Essays on the Literature of the French Enlightenment* (Cambridge: Cambridge University Press, 1987), pp.184-96.
65. L. Perfézou. *Beaumarchais: Le Mariage de Figaro* (Paris: Bordas, L'Œuvre au clair, 1989).
66. C. Petitfrère. *Le Scandale du Mariage de Figaro: Prélude à la Révolution française* (Brussels: Editions Complexe, 1989).
67. L. Puech. *Beaumarchais: Le Mariage de Figaro* (Paris: Nathan, Balises, 1990).
68. M. Viegnes. *Beaumarchais: Le Mariage de Figaro* (Paris: Hatier, Profil d'une oeuvre, 1991).

C. GENERAL STUDIES ON BEAUMARCHAIS

69. P. Larthomas. *Le Langage dramatique* (Paris: A. Colin, 1972).
70. —. 'Le style de Beaumarchais dans *Le Barbier de Séville* et *Le Mariage de Figaro*', *L'Information Littéraire*, 23 (1981).
71. G. Conesa. *La Trilogie de Beaumarchais: écriture et dramaturgie* (Paris: P.U.F. 1985).
72. R. Pomeau. *Beaumarchais ou la bizarre destinée* (Paris: P.U.F. 1987).
73. R. Robinson. 'La Musique des comédies de Figaro: éléments de dramaturgie', *Studies on Voltaire and the Eighteenth Century*, 275 (Oxford: Voltaire Foundation, 1990), 359-499.
74. Gunnar & Mavis Von Proschwitz. *Beaumarchais et le Courier de l'Europe*, 2 vols (Oxford: Voltaire Foundation, 1990). In vol. II, Document no. 613, 3 April 1793, pp.1147-48, we find Beaumarchais's comments on a performance of Mozart's opera *Le Mariage de Figaro*. He speaks of the acting and staging but not of the music for he was extremely deaf by this date. He has many suggestions for the final ballet and much advice for the actors.

D. STUDIES ON 'LE BARBIER DE SEVILLE' AS A BACKGROUND TO 'LE MARIAGE DE FIGARO'

75. John Dunkley. *Beaumarchais, Le Barbier de Séville* (London: Grant & Cutler, Critical Guides to French Texts, 86, 1991).

CRITICAL GUIDES TO FRENCH TEXTS

edited by
Roger Little, Wolfgang van Emden, David Williams